Stafford Hildred
and Tim Ewbank

martin Clunes

the biography

JOHN BLAKE

Published by John Blake Publishing Ltd,
3 Bramber Court, 2 Bramber Road,
London W14 9PB, England

www.johnblakepublishing.co.uk

www.facebook.com/Johnblakepub   facebook

twitter.com/johnblakepub   twitter

First published in hardback in 2010
This edition published in paperback in 2013

ISBN: 978-1-85782-802-3

British Library Cataloguing-in-Publication Data:

A catalogue record for this book is available from the British Library.

Design by www.envydesign.co.uk

Printed in Great Britain by CPI (UK) Limited

1 3 5 7 9 10 8 6 4 2

© Text copyright Stafford Hildred and Tim Ewbank 2013

Papers used by John Blake Publishing are natural, recyclable products made from
wood grown in sustainable forests. The manufacturing processes conform to the
environmental regulations of the country of origin.

Every attempt has been made to contact the relevant copyright-holders,
but some were unobtainable. We would be grateful if the
appropriate people could contact us.

Stafford Hildred: to Janet, Claire and Rebecca
Tim Ewbank: to Mollie New.
'Stranger, all you need is love'

CONTENTS

ACKNOWLEDGEMENTS

For their co-operation, help and encouragement, grateful thanks are due to: Roy and Liz Addison, Cindy Blanchflower, Peta Boreham, Vanessa Brooks, Alan Copley, Keith Cronshaw, Barbara Davis, Tom Duncan, Helen Fear, Carole Anne Ferris, Rod and Joy Gilchrist, June Hammond, Justine Harkness, Ken Hymas, Clive Jackson, Sian James, Jerry Johns, Paula Jones, Alan Kingston, Simon Kinnersley, Robert Kirby, Aidan MacEchern, Moira Marr, Barbara Molyneux, Denise Perry, Peter Radford, Alan Rawes, Alasdair Riley, Peter and Steve Sampson, Claire Sefton, Mike and Mabel Simmons, Lynn Trunley-Smith, Cynthia and Ian Warrington, Ros White.

The authors would like to acknowledge the TV programme *Comedy Connections* as an invaluable source of information. Additional important sources include *The Times*, *Sunday Times*, the *Express*, the *Sun*, the *Mirror*, the *Daily Mail*, *TV Times*, *Loaded*, *News of the World*, *Sunday Mirror*, *Best*, *Reveal*, *Now*.

Bibliography:
My Life Behaving Badly by Leslie Ash (Orion)
The Best of Men Behaving Badly by Simon Nye (Headline)
Alec Clunes by JC Trewin (Rockcliff)

CHAPTER 1

A CHIP OFF THE OLD BLOCK

'I suppose, like anyone, I had a deep-rooted need to be liked.
And it seemed that the easiest way to get someone to like
you was to make them laugh'
MARTIN CLUNES ON HIS DIFFICULT CHILDHOOD

After years of screen success, Martin Clunes has one of the most recognisable faces around. As an accomplished and versatile actor, he's won awards and acclaim for a long run of popular portrayals which have been seen all around the world.

While his hilarious performance as lager lout Gary in the long-running comedy series *Men Behaving Badly* might be among the best-remembered roles, he has also starred in films like *Saving Grace* and *Shakespeare in Love*, theatre classics such as Moliere's *Tartuffe* and turned stylish television series like *William and Mary* and *Doc Martin* into family favourites.

Somehow along the way he has also found time to develop successful parallel careers as a gifted director of films such as the hilarious *Staggered* and as a presenter of top-rated documentary series like his *Islands of Britain*.

But the simple, long-retired fisherman quietly mending a

neighbour's net outside his tiny cottage in a sleepy village on the western tip of Majorca has neither seen nor heard of a single one of those performances. Eighty-seven-year-old Pedro Garcia has no television and has never been to a cinema or even bought a newspaper or a magazine. Yet he remembers Martin Clunes very clearly, but only as a very young boy who became known to him and other villagers as 'the actor's son who is the fastest swimmer'.

The actor that Pedro recalls very fondly from the 1950s and 1960s – the days before the island was 'discovered' and changed forever by the arrival of millions of tourists on package holidays from all over Europe – was Martin's father, the highly distinguished Alec Clunes, then a very famous figure on stage and screen.

Pedro cheerfully admits he never saw Alec in dramatic action either, but he was fully informed of the level of the fame of Clunes Senior thanks to a well-educated friend in the nearby village of S'Arraco. Pedro's friend, a farmer called Gabriel, had travelled all over the world before settling down to run the family business, which included a small vineyard as well as the farm. Gabriel loved the theatre and was dazzled that such a big star would choose to spend his precious spare time in their quiet and rarely visited region.

Pedro will happily explain to anyone who takes the time to listen how Gabriel, who died in 2000, befriended Alec Clunes and his family. The actor and producer was at first cautious and a little withdrawn when he arrived. Majorca for

A CHIP OFF THE OLD BLOCK

Alec Clunes was very much an escape from a busy life with every day spent very much in the public eye.

For Martin's father, Majorca represented a chance to live simply, far from the reporters and photographers and the unwelcome trappings of celebrity. On the island he could forget who he had become and get right away from the daily pressures of life in London's theatreland and back to nature in his own piece of paradise.

To that end, he bought a tiny brick building which had previously been used to keep animals and set about making it habitable for himself and his family. 'It was a very difficult moment when Gabriel revealed that he knew of all the famous plays Alec Clunes had performed in,' Pedro said. 'He knew of the films and had read of the fine work as a producer, but this was not at all what the actor wanted to hear about. Gabriel was an honest man and he could not pretend that he knew nothing of the actor's great fame.

'But it created for a time a problem between them, until the actor realised that it made no difference to Gabriel who he was. Fame and fortune counted for nothing at that time in that quiet corner of the Mediterranean. Slowly the two men from completely different backgrounds became very good friends. On Majorca, Martin Clunes's father wanted to forget all about fame and the anguish of acting and just be an ordinary man, and Gabriel understood and accepted this.'

The locals saw the energetic and enterprising Alec Clunes throw himself into converting the remains of a derelict pigsty into a home and building and rebuilding nearby stone walls that had succumbed to years of decay, and they soon came to treat him as one of their own. 'He was just "the actor",' said Pedro. Alec brought his attractive wife Daphne to Majorca with him and it was in the warm bay of Sant Elm, or San Telmo as it was once better known, that their children – Martin and his older sister Amanda – learned to swim.

Both of them have precious childhood memories of blissful days in the sunshine while their famous father toiled happily like a labourer and their mother prepared delicious meals from local produce. Martin recalls that once they became old enough and safe enough in the water, they used to swim off with friends to the nearby rocky islets of Es Panteleu or Na Mitjana and sometimes, when they were a little older, to the larger island of Dragonera.

'We used to put picnics in plastic bags to keep them dry and just swim over for the day,' said Martin many years later. There was a freedom about those first holidays that Martin relishes to this day, and the children soon came to realise that the tough manual work was their father's way of relaxing. Martin reflected that his parents were 'hippies' and admitted happily that he too was a 'bit of a hippy at heart'.

The trip to Majorca as a young boy was Martin's first thrilling experience of life abroad and then it became a much-loved routine. 'I'd go with my family every school holiday,' Martin recalled. 'We made lots of friends and it was a cool place to holiday as a kid. We'd fly out on those old propeller planes and my dad had a way of exciting us about the trip to obscure any potential fear.'

A CHIP OFF THE OLD BLOCK

Before he went to Majorca, Martin's strongest memory of a family holiday was going to stay with his maternal grandparents in Sedlescombe in East Sussex. 'They used to take us down to the beach and we really loved it,' he said. But Majorca was magical and it was the start of Martin's great love of islands.

This was an idyllic time for Martin's father. He knew he had left fatherhood rather late in life because he was almost 50 by the time his son Alexander Martin, to give him his full name, arrived. But Alec was determined to do everything he could to make up for lost time and to make the most of every moment. He treasured the family time on the beautiful and then totally unspoiled island.

For hard-working Alec this was a chance for rare periods of rest and reflection towards the end of a long and extraordinary career, of which there are remarkable echoes in the life of his now celebrated son. Perhaps it also explains the family tradition of sustained artistic effort that helps to drive Martin Clunes to work so hard.

Alec Clunes, or Alexander de Moro Sherriff Clunes, to give him his full name, was born at 2 Western Road, Brixton, London on 17 May 1912. It was just a month after the supposedly unsinkable passenger liner *Titanic* hit an iceberg and went down, and as a nation Britain was still struggling to come to terms with the terrible tragedy.

Alec was himself born into a theatrical family. His father Alexander Sherriff Clunes was an actor of Cornish birth and Scottish descent, and his mother, Georgina Ada Sumner, was an actress who'd been born in Liverpool. Both had forged careers in the theatre without any previous history of acting in the family. In fact Alec's paternal grandfather was an architect who designed, among many other things, a hotel at Fowey in Cornwall.

But in spite of his parents' professional leaning, Martin's father did not originally intend to follow them on to the stage to earn his living. He first worked in advertising and journalism while acting only in amateur productions, but he had an obvious natural talent and by the time he was 22 he had made up his mind to turn professional. His first paid performance was as Orlando in Shakespeare's *As You Like It* at the Croydon Repertory Theatre. The *Croydon Advertiser* noted a 'sound performance, marred by monotonous cadences in delivery'. But Alec's raw talent was recognised and soon afterwards he was invited to join the Old Vic Company in London.

With his powerful voice and commanding presence, Alec Clunes' reputation as an actor of considerable talent and huge potential grew steadily. By 1939 he was one of the leading lights at the Shakespeare Memorial Theatre at Stratford upon Avon, where he played characters like Iago, Petruchio and Coriolanus with great success. He was now firmly established as a rising star and his prospects improved greatly after George Bernard Shaw saw him in action at the Malvern Festival and was deeply impressed.

Like Martin would be, Alec Clunes was a man of principle as well as talent. A dedicated pacifist, when World War Two broke out he flatly refused to join in the fighting. He risked his growing popularity as he became a conscientious objector and chose not to enlist in the forces. It was a bold decision that brought sneers and criticism and court appearances but he never flinched from it. Looking back, Martin recognises it took a great deal of courage for his father to do what he did. 'I'm full of admiration for the way he was brave enough to be a conscientious objector and face endless courts.'

Martin's dad was honest with the authorities and told them that he was an agnostic. So it was doubly hard for him, because he could not use religious convictions to spare himself from the conflict. He simply did not believe in taking up arms against other human beings, even if they were German invaders, and he said so publicly. Instead of fighting he did plenty of non-combatants' work like ambulance driving in the Blitz, which often put him in just as much danger as the troops in the front line. He also continued to act, starring in George Bernard Shaw's new play *In Good King Charles's Golden Days* and touring with the Old Vic.

When German bombs hit the headquarters of the Old Vic, the company moved to a temporary new home in the Lancashire town of Burnley and Alec Clunes went out to play Young Marlow, Malvolio and Taffy in *Trilby*. He also appeared in patriotic wartime films, most notably the well remembered *One of Our Aircraft is Missing*, which was released in 1942.

Perhaps the most important change in Alec Clunes' long career came in May 1942 when, back in London, he became an actor-manager, taking over the languishing Arts Theatre Club in Great Newport Street near Leicester Square. 'Because he was a conscientious objector, he found it very difficult to get work during and after the War,' Martin explained, 'so he took over the Arts Theatre.'

There were just 200 members when Alec Clunes founded the Arts Theatre Group of Actors, having raised capital of £1,500 (at that time a large sum of money). He was to serve inspirationally for the next 11 years as leading spirit, manager, director and actor. The theatre was generally doing not too badly financially during the War but its relative success was to a great extent due to revivals or tried and tested plays. Martin's dad was determined never to play safe. He resolved to use his new position to help new dramatists.

The young Peter Ustinov was completely unknown and serving as a private in the Army when Alec produced his play *House of Regrets*. At the premiere Ustinov answered calls for the author in full battle dress and within weeks the brilliant writer was dubbed 'the Chekhov of Baron's Court'. Ustinov remained forever grateful to his mentor. By the middle of 1944 the number of members at the Arts Theatre had risen to 13,000 as its reputation for high quality and challenging innovation grew and grew.

Martin's father earned enormous respect for using funds to help subsidise ambitious yet hard-up young dramatists whenever possible. For example, he helped Christopher Fry with money while he was writing *The Lady's Not For Burning* and then staged the play at the Arts Theatre in 1948 for two weeks with himself in the leading role.

Alec had commissioned Fry to write *The Lady's Not For Burning*, a romantic comedy set in the Middle Ages but reflecting the world's 'exhaustion and despair' following World War Two, with a war-weary soldier who wants to die and an accused witch who wants to live. Fry was only too happy to show his gratitude to Alec openly. 'At the front of the play are the words "For Alec Clunes",' Martin points out proudly.

The great left-leaning actor-producer would surely have been deeply unimpressed by Conservative Prime Minister Margaret Thatcher's memorable misquotation of the title at the 1980 Party Conference, 'You turn if you want to... the lady's not for turning.'

After the War Martin's father led an ambitious morale-boosting tour of Europe backed by the British Council. At the end of his fine performance as Hamlet in Prague, Alec spoke to the audience for about a minute in fluent Czech, which was such a happy surprise for the audience it brought the house down all over again. In Belgium there was a mix-up with the luggage labels, which led to his being nicknamed 'Monsieur Heavy Baggage' for some time.

By the time Alec Clunes left the Arts Theatre it had a membership of more than 25,000 and the company was thriving. Alec was always in demand and he played Hastings in Laurence Olivier's memorable film of *Richard III* (1955) and was also high in the cast list as the Duke of Burgundy in *The Adventures of Quentin Durward*.

Alec's marriage to the actress, and later businesswoman and television executive, Stella Richman had been dissolved in 1954. Two years later he married Martin's mother, a beautiful young woman called Daphne Acott, who had worked as a secretary to Orson Welles. The marriage produced two children, Amanda, now a writer, and Alexander Martin, now a man with a huge theatrical heritage to inspire him. Just before Amanda was born in 1959 Alec took over from Rex Harrison in the London stage version of *My Fair Lady*.

Martin was born on 28 November 1961, in a stylish two-storey, white-rendered Victorian family house next door to the well known Fox and Grapes public house on the edge of Wimbledon Common.

There is a strong facial similarity between Alec and Martin Clunes, and these days also a very marked similarity in their voices, according to some who remember Martin's father well. Although the father did not possess such prominent ears as Martin's, his lips, like those of his son, were often highlighted by reviewers seeking to paint a picture for their readers.

It is clear that had he lived longer, Alec Clunes would have been as big a star of television as he had been of the stage. He was offered the leading role of Professor Bernard Quatermass in the BBC's groundbreaking 1958 science-fiction serial *Quatermass and the Pit*, but he declined the part and Andre Morell was cast instead. Alec did still make several television appearances, including a major part in the classic 1950s adventure series *The Buccaneers*. One of his last roles was a character part in an early episode of the *Ronnie Barker Playhouse* in 1968.

Martin's early memories of his father are few because, as he points out, his dad worked largely in the theatre at night while Martin was tucked up in bed asleep at the family home. He does, however, remember being taken backstage at a theatre in London's West End where his father was appearing as the Archbishop of Canterbury in a play called *Soldiers*. The impression little Martin came away with was the gloominess and the dustiness of the set. But he did get to meet John Colicos, the Canadian actor playing Churchill. (Many years later Colicos would play Kor, the first Klingon commander *Star Trek: Deep Space Nine*.) That was a genuine thrill for a little boy like Martin and something he was later able to brag about to his friends.

Sadly Alec Clunes did not live long enough to make a huge impact on the small screen, nor to see any of his son's remarkable success in his own beloved profession. A heavy smoker who was often seen with a pipe in his mouth, Alec died from lung cancer on 13 March 1970. He was just 57.

Martin was only eight years old at the time and his father's death was clearly traumatic, but he has never been afraid to talk about his loss. 'We knew he was ill,' Martin remembered grimly many years later: 'He had the house in Majorca and was often away working, and this time he was away he was taken in to hospital. He actually fell ill in Majorca and was told by a doctor there that he had three days to live. So a family doctor and a friend went out and brought him back.

'When he came back the disease was diagnosed and he was given three weeks to live. In the event he died after three months, but it was pretty merciless. Fortunately, treatment for cancer has come a long way since then.'

Martin still recalls many details of the funeral. Although he was so young, he remembers everything about the day his father was cremated. He recalled to one interviewer how the wind caught the ashes just as they were being scattered, and how there was 'a long line of people being horrid to me, saying, "Go there, wear this, don't do that."' Martin said that at the crematorium he wanted to know what happened to the coffin and the handles. 'I remember Mum saying Dad liked a bit of wood in the bonfire – he was a keen gardener – so I wasn't troubled by it.'

As a young boy Martin grew up dreaming of becoming a milkman with his own float, but the early death of his father made him switch ambitions. He remembers seeing his father on stage a year before he died. 'I didn't want to act then, really,' Martin recalled to an interviewer. 'But I do believe that my father's death was very much a part of me wanting to do it. After Dad had died, when people asked me what I wanted to be when I grew up, I would say "an actor". I think I said it before I knew what it meant.' He added poignantly: 'My memories of my father are few and far off. Tiny, but reinforced by years, a bit like the chords you can remember to play on the guitar.'

After the death of his father Martin was sent off to be a weekly boarder at a prep school – Barfield School in

Farnham, Surrey. Founded in 1933, the school had an excellent reputation and it was felt that Martin would flourish there. But there was another reason for his becoming a boarder. There was a theory around at the time, he says, that if he remained at home being brought up with just a mother and a sister that he would turn out to be gay.

Martin does not have happy memories of being sent away to boarding school. 'It was horrible,' he said many years later. 'My father had just died. I was bullied by some of the older boys. And I was a bed wetter. It was a miserable time, but it just seemed like that was another of the shitty things one had to put up with being a child.' He tried to use humour to deflect the bullies and that helped a little. But he said grimly: 'I think I just laughed my way through. I mean, of course it all affected me, but you just do what you're told at that age. You're completely unempowered.'

Martin felt it was agony going away to school. It was a desperately sad time for his poor widowed mother as well. He would cry all the way there until his mum dropped him off and then she would shed tears all the way back. He could have been crushed and cowed after such an experience, but he wasn't. Indeed, whenever he recounts his schooldays he refuses pity. It wasn't all bad, he insists, and he certainly didn't snivel his way through school feeling rejected and shunned as an outcast or anything like that.

He was bullied, however, because he had arrived at the prep school from a state primary school and he found the posh Surrey boys were some way ahead of him in terms of confidence. But, he reflects, it was character building. 'Kids are barbaric – especially boys. I was called names, Big Ears, Dumbo – children will pick on anything that is different, but not having a father and being a bed-wetter were things which were picked out more.'

Bed-wetting is a hard problem to hide at a boarding school and it brought endless ribbing and ridicule from his contemporaries. At one point he was ordered to sleep in a room on his own on an incontinence mattress with an alarm attached under the sheet which sounded a bell whenever it got wet. It was a cripplingly embarrassing problem that instantly set him apart from the other boys.

At school Martin was not a boy who went looking for fights. They just tended to come to him. He recalled: 'These kids used to come up to me in the refectory, and hold these big trays on the sides of their heads and say, 'Oi Clunes, you big-eared ****!' I mean, you had to laugh. And if you could come back with something even funnier, that was even better.

'I suppose, like anyone I had a deep-rooted need to be liked. And it seemed that the easiest way to get someone to like you was to make them laugh. So I took all the piss-taking in my stride. Even when it got really cruel. This was shortly after my father had died, and these kids would take the piss out of me for not having a dad! I know that sounds completely barbaric, but that's how it was.'

Despite the tough times and the hard knocks, at no stage did Martin ask his mother to take him away from the school. That would have meant giving in. He has pointed out that as a child the natural thing was not to question the way his life was. 'You don't have any control of your destiny at that age – I certainly don't remember having any anyway.'

For years he fought to gain that control and says that therapy helped. 'It was years before the bed-wetting stopped. I went to see a shrink – it was all tied in with my dad's death and a sense of low self-worth. The shrink did work, but look at what I do for a living – I seek approval on a grandiose scale.'

Martin also cheerfully admits that he was a really annoying little boy. He was forever being caned for being an awful show-off, and he concedes he must have been every teacher's nightmare – a lippy, irritating child. But it was not quite all bad news, as one teacher had a big influence on him and helped to instil in him an emotion that he retains to this day – a profound love of animals.

Martin's school was set in acres of beautiful grounds, and apart from the well-maintained playing fields, there was an area reserved for a selection of animals including sheep, guinea pigs, chickens and rabbits. Teacher Mr Huggett gave young bed-wetter Martin the task of getting up every morning to let the animals out and then make sure they were safe at night. Mr Huggett's very act of entrusting Martin with some, albeit limited, care of the animals helped to give him a much needed feeling of self-worth among the other pupils. 'I got on so well with the animals,' Martin says fondly, 'and I still consider myself a bit of a bunny-hugger.'

But even today Martin cannot watch certain period dramas on television without feeling sad and car-sick because they remind him of the Sunday night serials of the time when his mother used to drive him back to school. But he knows himself well enough to understand that his difficult childhood experiences helped to account for his love for attention and applause or what he calls 'the actor's neediness, which I have in spades.'

With impressive frankness Martin has often explained that he was both a bully and a victim of bullies at school. 'But neither to any great or serious degree,' he qualifies. He was always a big boy for his age and was frequently being challenged to prove to other boys just how tough he thought he was. He concedes, however, that he was 'pretty naughty but in a rebel-without-a-cause sort of way'.

After Martin had found fame in *Men Behaving Badly*, Peter Davies, who was a teacher at Barnwell when Martin was a pupil, was asked for his memories. He was quoted as saying that Martin was 'certainly a personality' and added: 'In the school photograph of around 1973, everyone is sitting smiling and there is one character at the back pulling a silly face – and you can guess who that is.'

Although he does not see it as the most helpful of observations, Martin cites the best thing ever written on his school report were the seven words: 'Martin does not seem to bear grudges.' Nevertheless, those days are firmly in the past now and he has intimated that he has never thought about going back for a school reunion. 'It's just not on the agenda,' he has said.

Although Martin's early ambitions for a career flitted from

driving a milk float to becoming an astronaut or carpenter, seeing Peter O'Toole in the film *Murphy's War* when he was about nine was certainly a significant experience. 'It was set somewhere with lovely blue seas, and O'Toole's then real-life wife, Sian Phillips, played his love interest,' recalled Martin. 'Blue seas, blue skies, and real love – I thought, "That's gotta be the business for me."'

After four years at Barfield, when he was 13, Martin left to go to the Royal Russell School in Croydon. Founded in 1853, the co-educational school boasts a 110-acre parkland setting with an imposing mix of old and new buildings and, since it was within a half-hour reach of central London, it was deemed that Martin should attend as a day boy.

After the unhappy experiences at his prep school, Martin was relieved to be no longer boarding. But as a day boy he had to get up very early in the morning to catch the train down to Croydon and then take a bus from there to the school. For Martin, one of the great blessings of his move to the Royal Russell School in his adolescence was, he says, that it meant he did not have to look too far to find a person of the opposite sex.

In an interview with *Loaded* magazine, he said: 'They'd be sitting next to me in the classroom wearing those incredibly short skirts, which showed off their lightly tanned thighs rather nicely. However, sitting next to these girls and copping off with them were two very different things. I was always a good kisser. Of course I was blessed with an enormous set of lips, which undoubtedly helped. Actually,

I've always felt that the big tragedy of my life was that I was unable to snog myself!'

Martin reckoned, all things considered, that he fared reasonably well when it came to forming early attachments with girls, although he candidly confessed: 'I was never any good at the chatting up lark. In fact I've never chatted up a woman in my life. My policy was always to hang around a girl until I could think of something funny to say.' Fortunately for Martin, he had a good enough sense of humour to make sure this occurred frequently, which paid dividends.

As at Barfield, school and Martin were again not a smooth or easy mix. 'At 14 I came very close to being kicked out of school altogether,' he admits. 'I think I called my teacher "a bumbling incompetent fool".'

But there was at least one master at the Royal Russell whom Martin came to admire and like. His name was Andrew Foot and he was one of life's great enthusiasts, a man who seemed to see the positives in everything. Martin fondly remembers how he encouraged pupils to put on and take part in plays, and Mr Foot gave Martin a role in the school's production of *Love's Labours Lost* that the teacher directed.

Unfortunately there were also quite a few members of staff with whom Martin did not get on nearly so well. He was frequently getting into fights and often, even when he was not involved, he was irritated to find that he still managed to get the blame. By the time he reached his early teens he was already well over six feet tall, so he naturally stood out from his contemporaries and whenever any trouble was afoot it was always Martin Clunes who looked like a ringleader.

As Martin grew into a teenager, a degree of mischief also formed part of his behaviour in his home life at Wimbledon Common. Martin and his pals seized their chance to sit by the local golf course and dart out and snaffle balls when the golfers weren't looking. They would then trade them in at the local toyshop.

The Wombles were by no means the only people who had a good time on Wimbledon Common. Martin believes it was a great place to grow up. Most of his childhood memories recall time spent up trees smoking fags or making dens and learning to play the guitar while trying to fathom out the chords of Frank Zappa numbers. Martin's family was one of the last in his street to get a TV so he tended to spend more time on outdoor pursuits.

Climbing trees, smoking cigarettes and working out guitar chords on the Common were harmless enough. But as he told veteran reporter Pat Codd, 'I was forever being nabbed by our local bobby. We nicknamed him The Sheriff. He used to nick us kids for smoking in an alley.

'He would take us home to our mothers and say, "I know he's a good lad but…" Once he marched me home and my mother opened the door with our dog under her arm. The dog dribbled all over him, making a right mess. I thought, "That dog has got the right idea."'

On one occasion Martin's group of mates clambered into a battered old open-top VW Beetle for a smoke. The car had appeared to have been ditched in the station car park but they found the car keys in the glove compartment and although none of them could drive, they took it for a spin. Predictably they crashed the car with one of Martin's pals at the wheel.

'We got nicked once for riding a moped on a golf course on Wimbledon Common,' recalled Martin. 'We were jumping bunkers in it when we were caught by a park ranger.' On this occasion he escaped with a severe telling-off. A couple of years later Martin acquired his own moped and was exceedingly annoyed when it was stolen. His first proper motorbike was a Honda 250 – which, he says, also landed him in trouble with the local police in Wimbledon thanks to the absence of a tax disc.

'We often gave the staff in Kingston Hospital some grief,' Martin recounted to Pat Codd. 'We would race around in the wheelchairs with the porters chasing us. I don't think I was the easiest son. I was quite a lad. I was the one who was always beaten up by other gangs because I was the tallest and the slowest. They all wanted to prove how tough they were and I couldn't run because I smoked too much.'

The Sheriff once caught Martin setting fire to a large dustbin. 'Judging from his reaction you'd think he'd caught up with Carlos the Jackal and Lord Lucan all in one go,' said Martin. 'In retrospect, you would think he might have had better things to do with his time. Like solving the occasional crime, for instance. I got up to my fair share of mischief. I didn't exactly major in it, but I was always up for a laugh.'

A CHIP OFF THE OLD BLOCK

Sartorially, Martin went through some interesting periods, and was to be seen going around in huge flares until the arrival of the punk movement on the London scene in 1976, courtesy of the Sex Pistols, bondage gear, spiky Mohican haircuts, ripped T-shirts with safety pins, and spitting fans at riotous gigs pogo-ing frantically up and down.

'The biggest difference punk rock made to my life was that it gave me permission to behave appallingly,' Martin told *Loaded* magazine. 'It meant I could stop wearing flares and start wearing black drainpipe trousers. Also it meant that I could get a half-decent haircut. I remember going to school on a Monday morning after getting my first "punk" cut. I thought I looked like the ultimate street rebel. As I walked through the school gates, a teacher walked past and said, "Good haircut, Clunes." Which of course was the last thing I wanted to hear.'

Susan Ballion, better known as punk singer Siouxie Sioux of The Banshees, was a particular favourite of Martin's. But until punk came along, Martin had always been a fan of Chuck Berry, one of the truly great pioneers of blues-rock. He had first got into Chuck Berry in 1972 shortly before his 12th birthday, when he was one of thousands of youngsters who went out and bought Chuck's controversial hit record *My Ding-a-Ling* and helped push it to the top of the UK charts.

My Ding-a-Ling was anything but the kind of record with a rocking riff for which Berry was famous. In fact it was a novelty song laden with double entendres about playing with his 'ding-a-ling'. Chuck tried to pretend his 'ding-a-ling' was just two silver bells on a string given to him by his grandmother, which he played with in school, and grabbed on to in tight situations such as falling off a wall or swimming across a creek infested with snapping turtles. But, like Martin, everyone who sang along to the lyrics knew exactly what Chuck meant by his 'ding-a-ling'. Especially when clean-up-the-airwaves campaigner Mary Whitehouse condemned the BBC for playing a record containing such vulgarity.

Martin remembers that when he brought the record home and his mother heard it, she too disapproved and considered it rude which, Martin concedes, indeed it was. And on the strength of that, Martin says, he went out and bought a compilation LP of Chuck Berry's greatest hits, believing it would be brimming with more thinly disguised songs about the male sexual organ. 'But to my great disappointment it wasn't,' he told *Loaded*. 'It was all *Too Much Monkey Business* and *Johnny B. Goode*. Nothing about knobs at all,' he laughed.

In his early teens, while many of his pals were pulling girls and having what appeared to be the time of their lives, Martin described his own relationships with the opposite sex as 'a constant source of torture.' He was not a babe magnet, even before the term was invented. Martin recalls that he never really had a particular type of girl that he went for, but he did have a crush on Farrah Fawcett Majors, the American actress who became an international sex symbol as Jill Munroe in the hit TV series *Charlie's Angels*.

A picture of a pouting Farrah with lustrous, tumbling blonde locks and her curvy body squeezed tightly into a red swimming costume became an iconic pin-up photograph and poster in the mid-1970s, and a small copy of it was regularly tucked into the wallet of the teenage Martin. Until Farrah shone out from the television screen, it was a picture of another archetypal blonde fantasy sex kitten, French siren Brigitte Bardot, sitting suggestively astride a motorcycle, that fired Martin's teenage male imagination. 'I used to try to convince myself that she was saving herself for me,' Martin owned up. 'But, apart from those two, the kind of women I've always been drawn to are the ones that like me.'

Martin did attempt to make himself appear more grown up and attractive to the opposite sex when he was about 15 by getting a job on a passing funfair on Wimbledon Common. He thought by becoming a dodgem car operator he would be able to impress the girls with the offer of a free ride or two. 'I used to try to look as macho as I could,' Martin recalled of his job shepherding people into the bumper cars and making sure the doors were shut. But unfortunately Martin's macho posing extended to a hefty kung fu kick on a passing dodgem to try and make it spin, which only resulted in the humiliation of a broken bone in his foot. He felt an utter chump, because not only did this bring that particular career to a painful and sudden end but it singularly failed to impress any of the watching girls.

To earn himself a bit of money, Martin also took a Saturday job in a wine store in Wimbledon where he stacked shelves and sorted out boxes of bottles in the shop's downstairs storeroom. There he was able to avail himself of a liberal helping of Stone's ginger wine even though, he says, he was under 16.

Sadly, the aforementioned enthusiasm of schoolmaster Mr Foot failed to rub off on Martin and he left school with just one O level and a solitary CSE. 'My best subject was going home,' he admitted later. 'Oh, and keeping a very close observation on the clock. My worst subject was turning up.

'I think teachers despaired of me,' he said. 'I certainly wasn't the sort of young man who belonged to clubs or societies. I wasn't any good at games either and I'm still not. I was just totally disinterested.'

CHAPTER 2

FIRST STEPS

'I watched myself again recently and I was awful, just awful'
MARTIN ON HIS TV DEBUT IN DOCTOR WHO

By the time he was 16 Martin might not have acquired too many qualifications, but he had learned that he would like to be an actor. His experience so far was minimal – a role as an Eskimo in a school nativity play and, as we have seen, a part in *Love's Labours Lost* at the Royal Russell School.

Predictably, the advice at school was that although acting might be a fun career, it might also be advisable to have something else to fall back on. But Martin was actively encouraged by his mother Daphne to follow in the footsteps of his father, and she was pleased when her son managed to win a place at the Arts Educational drama college in Chiswick, west London.

The Arts Educational has had many famous students through its doors, from Nigel Havers to Julie Andrews, and following his own success Martin is now very proud to be a Trustee. But during his time there he was never one of

25

its more studious pupils. 'I was a proper brat,' he once said. 'Most of the people in my classes were very serious about their training, but I treated it all as a bit of a joke. During one production of a Greek tragedy I squirted everyone in the chorus with a water pistol when the director was not looking.'

When he was about 18 years old, Martin was shocked to learn that his impressions of the happy family living an apparently blessed life in their big house on Wimbledon Common and spending long lazy summers in Majorca were far from the whole story.

He discovered that in fact his father had separated from his mother and had been living in Majorca at the time the cancer struck. Martin had had no idea that the marriage was in any trouble. 'He had left us,' Martin told an interviewer. 'At the time I didn't know. Mum kept it from us.' That had not been so difficult as Alec Clunes never worked a nine-to-five job. He was an actor, often working far away from home, so there had always been 'a degree of absenteeism' there.

'The cancer was diagnosed not long after,' said Martin. 'And not long after that, he was dead. For years, I never talked to my mother about it, but I know she was wounded massively. It could have got better, you see. They could have resolved it, maybe, but then he died so there was always that sense of unfinished business.'

Martin was shattered by the news. It was hard enough to lose your father when you're still a young boy but growing up and discovering that your father had walked out on the family is a tough thing to handle. 'I did talk about it with Mum once,' said Martin. 'She said, "I always thought he left me," meaning that it was in some way her fault. I said, "Actually, he left us all." And that is what sucks to me.'

But Martin's mother also had an enthusiasm for the entertainment business. Daphne had worked for the acclaimed writer, actor, producer and director Orson Welles before Martin was born. She had been hugely inspired by her multi-talented, ebullient boss who directed and starred in *Citizen Kane*, one of the greatest movies of all time.

Daphne had worked for Welles soon after she'd left art school and her tales of being employed by the brilliant yet incredibly demanding American had long since passed into Clunes family folk lore. Martin had heard all the extraordinary stories of his mother's experiences with the genius many times but he still loved to re-tell them.

He would slip easily into the famous sonorous voice, the authoritative tones that panicked the whole of pre-television America in 1938 with a vivid radio version of the *War of the Worlds*. (Younger readers might remember them in 'Probably the best lager in the world' in the famous Carlsberg commercial.) 'Welles was massive but he could move silently, apparently.' Martin would recall. 'He would suddenly appear and give Mum a £10 note and say, "Daphne, go and see how few cigars you can buy."'

Daphne delighted in telling how Welles would just check out of a hotel in Paris without packing or paying and leave her to go through the drawers, in which she would find unused plane tickets, cash, bills and other assorted personal documents. His mother's memories were an early lesson in the problems of Hollywood excess. 'America does that to people in this industry,' said Martin.

A much more direct influence on Martin was the popular actor Jeremy Brett, best known for his television portrayal of Sherlock Holmes in the mid-1980s, who was his mother's first cousin. 'Jeremy Brett was wonderful,' said Martin. 'He made you feel like a million dollars when you were with him. He was a big influence on my life, a bigger influence than I had realised.'

Martin's mother had been very close to Brett when they were younger. She was only two or three years older than him, and when he was at Eton she used to go and take him out to the cinema and they would sit and watch two films in a day. 'Then, when he was doing *War and Peace* in Venice, with Henry Fonda and Audrey Hepburn, he was living with Robert Graves' daughter,' said Martin. 'It was all so terribly glamorous. He was so encouraging and positive.'

As Martin left drama school, Brett arrived back from Hollywood to play Sherlock Holmes. He had mainly been in Los Angeles since Martin and his sister had been small children but he took an interest in his relatives and was very supportive in many ways. He even offered to pay for Martin to have his ears pinned back. 'He was always a great giver of love and support, as was his family,' said Martin, 'and there he was with his chequebook.' Martin did consider the procedure for a moment but decided against it. 'You stand in the mirror, hold them back and think, "That doesn't really fix it, does it?" Because the truth is: "I'm so vain I don't want anyone to think I am vain." I'm very good at hiding it.'

But Martin never hides his admiration for Brett. 'He was the dad in my business that I never had,' he says. 'I knew he was there for me, always.'

Later, in 1992, Martin did a play that toured war-torn Yugoslavia, and while he was in Belgrade he had to fly to Prague to play a Nazi in a Disney film called *Swing Kids*. When Martin got to Belgrade airport it was full of children dressed in camouflage and the flight was delayed for four hours with no explanation. Martin found it a strange, lonely time and slightly unnerving. Then he managed to find a bar with a television and it happened to be showing Sherlock Holmes starring, of course, Jeremy Brett. At such a bleak time Martin could draw some comfort from seeing Jeremy's familiar face twinkling at him from the TV set, even though he was speaking Serbo-Croat.

Martin might not have been the most obviously promising pupil at Arts Educational, but he did find paid employment pretty quickly when he left the college. He started out in fortnightly repertory and at the age of 19 made his professional debut in a Dorothy L Sayers play called *Busman's Holiday* at the Mercury Theatre in Colchester.

The theatre was relatively new, having opened just six years before, and Martin trod the boards there for the first time as PC Tom Sellon. He found the experience exciting and just as importantly, he also felt comfortable on stage, and during his stint in rep he learned a great deal.

Martin's early foray into rep was also memorable for an accident that seriously limited his mobility for a while. One night he was larking about in the early hours and injured his foot. Martin's hazy recollection of the incident was that he was out chasing the moon, tripped over a rabbit burrow and broke a bone in his foot. 'They couldn't set my foot in time so I soldiered on in the JB Priestley play *When We Are Married* on crutches,' he remembers.

The irony was that the local press heaped great praise upon the crippled young actor for having courageously lived up to his profession's rallying cry that the show must go on. It was, of course, priceless publicity for the play and drew an extra number of theatre-goers wanting to see such triumph-over-pain heroism on stage. 'Fortunately no one realised how irresponsible I'd been getting injured in the first place,' Martin has since admitted. 'At the time my life was like one long stag night and I would often wake up in the morning wishing the night before had never happened.'

As is so often the case, overnight success as an actor took a while to arrive and when acting work failed to roll in Martin was prepared to turn his hand to other ways of earning a living. He was paid £15 for agreeing to pose for the then little-known oddball artists Gilbert and George. Their work now fetches hundreds of thousands of pounds.

'It was only half an hour's work,' said Martin. 'I had just left college and I was skint. I didn't know who Gilbert and

George were. I just got picked to do it. It was all very easy. I just had to sit there. Gilbert and George dressed identically and were very charming and polite.'

George recalled using Martin and said: 'A lot of young people used to model for us. We were introduced to Martin by one of our friends so we decided to ask him and he said yes straight away and seemed absolutely thrilled. Martin was not well known then, but I do remember that he was a very nice person.' Martin is featured in two Gilbert & George works, *World* and *Mouth*.

Success might seem to have come easily to the young Martin Clunes, but in fact there was a period of about 18 months in the early 1980s when he was out of work. It was a difficult time and Martin found himself seriously questioning if acting really was the right choice of career. In fact he became quite uncomfortable with the very idea of being an actor. 'I used to think it was quite a useless, stupid job for a grown man,' he told an interviewer. 'I couldn't reconcile myself to it at all.'

His attitude changed completely once he started directing and took a play to Nigeria. Just doing workshops with African actors and students made him realise that acting was far from 'useless'. 'It won't heal, house or feed anyone,' he said, 'but these people seemed to get so much from it. In Nigeria, on any street corner, you will find people using theatre as a kind of news vehicle or for exchanging opinions.

'After that experience acting for a living did not gain any more importance in my mind, but I found it to be as important

31

as it is. It's much more satisfying when you are clear about what you've got to offer and what the job has to offer you.'

Work started to come more regularly to the gawky kid with the big ears. His first television job, at the age of 20, was in a BBC *Play for Today* adaptation of the Russian writer Mikhail Bulgakov's novel *The White Guard* in 1982. That was followed the next year by an appearance in the BBC's hit series *Doctor Who,* wearing a rather feminine-looking blue satin outfit as the sinister Prince Lon. It was during the period when Peter Davison played the time traveller and Lon was the ruler of an outer-galactic planet. 'I was the villain and I had to wear a skirt,' Martin laughed. 'I got to be the guest baddie for four weeks and it was great.'

Great at the time, that is. These days Martin is embarrassed by the memory. Not so long ago he admitted to a journalist: 'I watched myself again recently and I was awful, just awful. For some reason because I was a prince I pronounced "S" as "sh". Soon everyone else seemed to be doing it too. It seemed to be infectious on this planet!' When it was suggested that the episodes in question surely deserve to be collector's items, Martin just looked horrified and said: 'That's just it – they are!'

At least he was able to use the fee for his *Doctor Who* appearance to help splash out on a three-litre BMW, in which he felt very grand, especially compared with the Hillman Minx which had been his first car and the much flashier bright red Audi 100 which superceded it. Martin had never taken any driving lessons, but he had still managed to pass his driving test first time at the age of 17, such was his natural aptitude for cars and motorbikes.

Close friends of Martin always mention his remarkable resourcefulness at all times. He illustrates the point perfectly when he recalls: 'I once found myself in a difficult situation when I had to get a plane from Majorca to England at the last minute. I couldn't afford to get a flight, so I tricked an official at Palma Airport into getting me home for free by saying that my father had died. It wasn't entirely a lie, but it had happened 11 years previously.'

Martin's distinctive looks have always made it just about impossible to mistake him for anyone else. He is 6ft 3in tall and with his large ears and fleshy features, he cheerfully says himself that he has a 'funny' face. 'I've been called all sorts of things,' he laughs. 'I've been described as "a cross between a telegraph pole and a Bash Street Kid" and someone once said I had "a face like a torn arse".'

Perhaps the worst comment came soon after *Doctor Who* when he played Mark Antony in a production of *Julius Caesar* at the Open Air Theatre in Regent's Park, London. The now-defunct magazine *City Limits* really put the boot in and said: 'Martin Clunes as Mark Antony is spiritually and physically repulsive.' Martin philosophically shrugged off such gratuitous insults but said his mother didn't like them.

Apparently there was much sniggering from the audience when Mark Antony came to his memorable speech: 'Friends, Romans, countrymen, lend me your ears…'

CHAPTER 3

LOVE AND MARRIAGE

'Friends told me it was unlucky to wear green
at a wedding, but I didn't listen'
LUCY ASTON ON HER MARRIAGE TO MARTIN CLUNES

Paul McCartney has said that the Beach Boys' *God Only Knows* is the most beautiful love song ever written. Since its release in 1966, Brian Wilson's masterpiece has become one of the most popular wedding songs of all time. Its gorgeous melody and touching message of love have had a profound effect on thousands of young lovers down the years, among them Martin Clunes and Lucy Aston.

Martin and Lucy, a pretty blonde actress he had fallen for, had just spent a couple of very happy hours at a Beach Boys concert at Wembley, listening to the group running through their extensive hits including *God Only Knows*, when Martin decided he had something important to tell his girlfriend. 'I remember Lucy was in the bath and I simply said to her, "Will you marry me?"'

'Her eldest sister was married to the drummer of the Beach Boys and lived in Los Angeles,' Martin said. 'I'd met all of Lucy's family. He was the last one I'd met and we'd had such a great time at the concert I thought, "I've met them all now. Time to pop the question!"' Lucy accepted Martin's proposal of marriage without hesitation. She was madly in love with him.

Martin's romance with the beef farmer's daughter from Kent had begun when they were both cast in a touring production of JM Barrie's play *The Admirable Crichton*, starring Rex Harrison and Edward Fox. But the path to love was not exactly smooth. 'I thought she was lovely,' said Martin, 'but I was living with someone else.'

At that point Lucy was better known than Martin was. A product of the Italia Conti stage school, Lucy had first made a good impression when she played a key role in *By the Sword Divided*, the BBC's lavish costume drama series about the English Civil War, screened in 1983. She was already entrancing viewers as the spirited Lady Lucinda Ferrar around the time Martin was making his TV debut in *Doctor Who*.

The driving force behind *By the Sword Divided* was John Hawkesworth, whose outstanding list of credits as a writer and producer of top quality TV drama included such gems as the Emmy award-winning international hit *Upstairs, Downstairs*, the period drama *The Duchess of Duke Street* and the mini-series *The Flame Trees of Thika*.

Hawkesworth was drawn to the subject of England's 17th-century Civil War by his personal family tree, which revealed that his own ancestors had fought on opposing sides. The result was *By the Sword Divided*, a sweeping costume drama that focused on the conflicts and torn loyalties within a single family at that time.

Lucy won a role in this prestigious series as feisty Lucinda Lacey, the younger daughter of the family central to the series. The Laceys lived in Arnescote Castle, and viewers saw Lucinda grow up to become Lady Lucinda Ferrar upon marriage, and blossom into a very single-minded, passionately driven young woman who throws herself so vigorously and deeply into the Royalist cause that at one point she refuses to speak to her sister Anne.

Lucy's fiercely independent character was, perhaps predictably, referred to as a 'lusty lass' but Lucy acquitted herself well over 17 episodes of the drama, which contained adultery, treachery, murder, as well as blood and thunder as the conflict deepened.

With its bonnets and bustles, betrayal and butchery, *By the Sword Divided* won a devoted following in Britain. A television series of this pedigree naturally sold well to other countries around the world, including America, where audiences received it warmly. All of this gave Lucy something of an international profile at a time when Martin had yet to get a meaningful foothold on British TV. Friends of the couple were adamant, however, that Martin was not in the slightest bit envious of the fact. On the contrary, he was very pleased for her and fully supportive.

Lucy had followed *By the Sword Divided* with other stage and TV roles, including an appearance in *C.A.T.S. Eyes*, the

ITV detective drama series which starred, among others, Leslie Ash – with whom Martin would team up in *Men Behaving Badly* just a few years later.

Now, in the summer of 1986, Lucy was teamed with Martin Clunes in the stage play *The Admirable Crichton*. Prophetically, Martin and Lucy were cast as lovers, and audiences witnessed the couple getting engaged on stage every night. As sometimes happens in the couple's profession, life imitated art.

Lucy found herself warming to Martin early on in rehearsals. She found him sweet, shy, somewhat vulnerable, full of energy and terrific fun. Their relationship became something more than just professional on-stage affection when the production moved to Bath. The couple were sharing a cottage in Wales with other cast members, but their relationship moved on to another level when they found themselves alone one weekend after their housemates had returned to London.

When *The Admirable Crichton* moved into London's West End and opened at the Theatre Royal on 8 August 1988, Martin was based in a house in Brixton which he shared with another actress, but he began spending nights at Lucy's flat in Crouch End in north London. It was a confusing time emotionally for the young actor as he struggled to find where his true affections lay, a quest made all the more difficult by getting engaged to Lucy on stage every night.

The play closed in December after a four-month run, and it seemed that Lucy's and Martin's relationship off stage was not to be matched by the nightly on-stage conclusion. The couple went their separate ways but remained friends, albeit somewhat awkwardly. Lucy bought a garden flat in Tufnell Park, north London, where she resolved to get on with her life anew.

But when Lucy started working on a new production, Martin turned up on the first night, clearly having sorted out his emotions and where his heart lay. Lucy's recollection is of Martin declaring theatrically: 'I can't be without you. I love you too much to be without you.' According to Lucy, 'It was the most wonderful, romantic thing anyone had ever said to me. I took him home and he never moved out.'

As Martin began to pick up roles in TV and Lucy's career continued to flourish, life was looking good for the young couple. And two years later, after their night with the Beach Boys, came Martin's proposal of marriage. The couple set a date for a spring wedding in 1990 in the parish church of St. Mary's in Chilham, where Lucy had been christened. Situated between the Kent cities of Canterbury and Ashford, Chilham is the most picturesque of villages, noted for its olde worlde charm and beauty which attracts hundreds of tourists every year.

It boasts a fine castle at the end of its delightful village square, all of which was seen to good effect as the alluring backdrop to the BBC's drama serial adaptation of Jane Austen's *Emma*. Chilham is a perfect setting for a traditional wedding, and Martin and Lucy made plans to tie the knot at the village's imposing Norman church. Steeped in history, it was built on land once owned by an Anglo-Saxon called Sired, who fought for King Harold at the Battle of Hastings, and is mentioned in the Domesday book in 1086.

Lucy decided to design her own dress for her wedding, and chose a gown with layers of white velvet and an emerald underskirt. According to her friends, she was tempting the fates by wearing green at her wedding because it was said to be unlucky. But she went ahead anyway, dismissing their worries as mere superstition, something which she would ponder later.

Lucy made a radiant bride, and among the guests at the wedding were actress Sharon Maughan, who had played her sister Anne in *By the Sword Divided*, and Tim Bentinck, who had played her brother Tom Lacey in the same serial.

Afterwards, in a nod to Martin's London roots, the couple were driven through the tree-lined lanes of Kent in a London black cab to spend their first night as man and wife at Chilston Park, an elegant 17th-century Grade 1 listed manor house hotel set in 23 acres of glorious rolling Kent countryside.

As Martin was rehearsing for his role as Mark Antony in Shakespeare's *Julius Caesar* in Regent's Park, he was given just three days off to get married before being required to report for work again. The plan was for the couple to spend just their wedding night at Chilston Park and then drive down to Mousehole in Cornwall the following day. But when they woke up in the morning, Mousehole seemed an awfully long way away. It would mean a very long, tiring drive, and as

Martin's time off from *Julius Caesar* was so limited, they asked if they could remain at Chilston Park for the extra nights.

The management could hardly refuse a request from such a charming and delightful just-married couple, and they readily agreed to accommodate the newlyweds for extra nights, even though it meant some switching around of rooms. Martin and Lucy weren't complaining. They were just happy and grateful to be able to stay. 'We were moved to a different room each night,' said Martin. 'It was perfect. At night they turned off electric light and used nothing but candles – very romantic.'

Their brief honeymoon was over all too quickly and the couple headed back to London, where Martin picked up where he had left off preparing for his Mark Antony role in Regent's Park. Martin may not have set the world of theatre alight in this particular production of *Julius Caesar* but he was at least able to come away with one highly amusing memory.

During one performance of the play at the Open Air Theatre it began raining hard just as Martin was staggering on stage with Caesar's limp body in his arms. He had just laid the corpse of the great Roman Emperor on the floor when there came an announcement over the tannoy system, asking the actors to kindly leave the stage because of the downpour – whereupon the supposedly lifeless Caesar rose to his feet and walked off. 'It kind of spoiled the magic!' Martin chuckled.

The newlyweds had a seemingly bright future to look forward to. Their stars appeared to be rising as actors and they were able to afford a decent lifestyle without too many money worries.

Friends of the couple could see that Lucy clearly adored her husband. 'Her great quality is that she loves me,' Martin acknowledged. 'That's a great plus.' He conceded, however, that he was not one for wearing his heart so openly on his sleeve. 'I am a romantic at heart,' he said, 'but all too frequently I forget. The feeling is all there but I often don't demonstrate it. But it's all right because she always says: "Get me some flowers!" She's absolutely right!'

Lucy's flat, with its stripped wooden floors and rambling garden, was a comfortable and fashionable first home for the couple, and they soon acquired two dogs and a cat to keep them company. Starting a family was most certainly on their agenda. Lucy went so far as to ask her agent to pick acting jobs which were based in London because she wanted to be able to stay at home and look after the child they were planning to have.

The animals helped to give their home a feeling of cosy domesticity, and Martin, always a dab hand at carpentry – he has said he is really a frustrated cabinet-maker – weighed in with some DIY improvements to the kitchen, including making a sideboard.

'My wife is a brilliant cook,' Martin said two years into his marriage, 'but she won't let me cook without watching over my shoulder – which drives me mad.' In time Lucy became a vegetarian, which, Martin revealed to one of the authors, caused some culinary problems. 'I married a beef-farmer's daughter who is now turning vegetarian,' he protested mildly. 'She's given up eating meat but I say: "Look, you married a meat-eating smoker, so leave me alone."

'I had a nutburger,' he added with a grimace, 'and it kept me awake all night. I enjoy the odd fart now and then, but this was the cubic capacity of a Rover each time for about four hours and I couldn't sleep!' It was said in jest, but it was a small indication of the bigger picture in Martin's and Lucy's marriage. They were changing, and now neither of them was sure they were really on the same path.

The nutburger remark, however, could have come from the lips of a certain Gary Strang, a character whom Martin was starting to come to grips with for a new TV sitcom for which he had high hopes. It was called *Men Behaving Badly*.

CHAPTER 4

MEN BEHAVING BADLY

*'A top-heavy 18-year-old aerobics instructor
who owns an off-licence'*
GARY STRANG'S IDEA OF HIS IDEAL WOMAN,
ACCORDING TO HIS GIRLFRIEND DOROTHY

On the face of it, Simon Nye was an unlikely creator of
Men Behaving Badly, the sitcom about a couple of
lovable lager louts which became the defining TV comedy of
the 1990s. Nye had studied French and German at London
University and begun his writing career as a translator
working on books on such cultural luminaries as Wagner
and Matisse.

Then, as Nye vividly remembers, after a fireworks party in
1984, he sat down and began writing his first novel, called
Men Behaving Badly. It was few years before it was published
and, although it didn't exactly set the world on fire, it caught
the eye of TV producer Beryl Vertue. At first she thought it
could be turned into a film but, as the book didn't have a
clear ending, she decided it could be better developed as a
television series.

In 1990 Beryl tracked Nye down to the Credit Suisse bank

where he was working as a translator and asked him if he could adapt his novel for the small screen. Coming from someone as successful and well respected in the television industry as Beryl, this was an offer Nye could hardly refuse. But, as a precaution, he still kept up the day job.

Beryl had originally been a secretary for the celebrated scriptwriters Ray Galton and Alan Simpson, who created *Steptoe and Son*, the BBC sit-com launched in 1962 that became one of the all-time comedy greats. She then became an agent representing a number of comedy writers including Spike Milligan, Eric Sykes, Johnny Speight, Galton and Simpson, as well as top comedy stars Tony Hancock and Frankie Howerd.

Beryl then became executive producer for the film versions of three BBC TV hit comedies by her stable of writers, *Till Death Us Do Part*, *Up Pompeii* and *Steptoe and Son*, along with The Who's rock opera *Tommy*, before striking out as a producer on her own. By the time Nye's *Men Behaving Badly* novel came to her attention, Beryl's track record was extremely impressive except in one area – she had never produced a sit-com. *Men Behaving Badly* would be untried territory for both herself and Nye.

Beryl picked up on Nye's book shortly after she had struck out on her own. In an interview about the value of small independent production companies, she later revealed: 'When I found the idea of *Men Behaving Badly* I was a company of one. I had my office in Shepperton Studios and I had Shepperton Studios on my notepaper so I looked more important. But if I'd had a company of 50 people I might have missed it because I wouldn't have had the time.'

With a few notable exceptions like *Rising Damp* and *The New Statesman*, ITV's recent track record in situation comedy had been mediocre. But it was to ITV that Beryl took her idea of a *Men Behaving Badly* series. She approached John Howard Davies, then head of entertainment at Thames TV which held ITV's weekday broadcasting franchise for the London area.

Beryl simply gave him Nye's book to read and, as Davies has happily admitted, he said he would do so and get back to her in three months – a lengthy deadline deliberately conjured up to try to deter her. 'I had enough scripts to read so I wasn't into reading books,' he explained.

On reading the novel Davies felt it was disjointed and he told Beryl he didn't quite see the potential in it that she so clearly did. But to Beryl's great surprise, he thought enough of her and her judgement to give his blessing to go ahead. Beryl took it as a huge compliment, but at the same time she found the responsibility quite unnerving.

Nye's *Men Behaving Badly* book and scripts centred on four characters: laddish Gary Strang who takes in a lodger, Dermot Povey, to help pay the mortgage on his flat, Gary's long-suffering girlfriend Dorothy, a feisty nurse, and Deborah, a sexy blonde singleton and fantasy girl lusted after by both boys after she moves into the flat she has bought upstairs.

To secure a commission from ITV, the project required a bankable star name, so the powers that be were more than happy when Harry Enfield, whom Beryl knew well, agreed to play Dermot the lodger. Harry had first made his name on Channel 4's *Saturday Live* programme by creating a number of memorable funny characters. Among them were Stavros, a Greek restaurant owner struggling with his impossibly fractured English, Tory Boy, a pompous Conservative MP, and the loudmouth Loadsamoney, an obnoxious braggart constantly boasting of the size of his 'wad' – the amount of money he was earning.

Enfield's characters had quickly entered the national consciousness, and by the time he came to *Men Behaving Badly*, the chameleon-like Harry was hot comedy property. He was a firm TV favourite who made millions laugh. On screen he slipped seamlessly from one guise to another, but it remained to be seen whether he could carry a six-episode sitcom playing just one character. *Men Behaving Badly* represented a significant shift in direction for him.

Harry was the first to be cast and Martin had the good fortune to be teamed with him after Enfield had seen him on the London stage and subsequently roped him in on some of his TV sketches. The two had worked well together and they had also gelled in *Gone to the Dogs*, an ITV comedy drama about dog racing which featured Martin as a bungling accountant called Pilbeam.

Although they had got on well both on and off screen, Martin still needed some considerable convincing before he was prepared to sign up for *Men Behaving Badly*. He was reluctant to commit to another TV sitcom after his experiences in *No Place Like Home* and *All at Number 20*, which, although enjoyable in themselves, had not proved to be of great benefit in developing his range as an actor or advancing his career significantly. According to Martin, it took four hours of persuasive talk from Harry Enfield, during which the two pals demolished a bottle of brandy, before he was finally persuaded. Harry was convinced that this was the role that really could be the making of Martin.

Caroline Quentin, in the role of Gary's long-suffering girlfriend Dorothy, came to *Men Behaving Badly* having enjoyed a similarly varied acting career but without as yet becoming a big name. The youngest of four girls from Reigate in Surrey, Caroline had left school at 16 with her heart set on a showbiz career and taken her first step in a seaside variety show at Lowestoft as 'one of those girls who stand in the background with sparkly bikinis on'. Years of rep and many months out of work had followed before Caroline's perseverance paid off. She gravitated towards the alternative comedy scene before going on to make her sit-com debut in *Don't Tell Father*. This now forgotten BBC series starred Tony Britton as a pompous actor with Caroline playing the daughter whose boyfriend he disapproves of. The alternative comedy scene was starting to flourish and, for Caroline, *Men Behaving Badly* was initially what she perceived as just another casting call. She auditioned for the role of Dorothy and was called back twice before being offered what was to be a career-making part.

With Harry, Martin and Caroline on board, only the role

of Deborah remained to be cast. But there was only ever going to be one actress who would be considered for the part. When Simon Nye was writing his novel he had always had in his mind Leslie Ash when dreaming up the gorgeous fantasy girl living upstairs from the boys, so when it came to casting Deborah for the TV show there were no other contenders. Nye was moved to describe her as 'the prettiest woman in Britain' and the admiring male following she picked up as the lovely Harmony hairspray girl in the 1978 advertisements would not disagree.

Leslie had enjoyed a successful career which had started when she was four years old, asking 'Mummy, why are your hands so soft?' in an advertisement for Fairy Liquid. Leslie went on to play the romantic lead in the movie musical *Quadrophenia* and to co-present the pop music show *The Tube*. She also co-starred – as computer wizard crimefighter called Fred Smith who worked for an all-female detective team – in 30 episodes of the drama series *C.A.T.S. Eyes*, ITV's much less glossy answer to America's *Charlie's Angels*.

Leslie's combination of solid TV experience and a natural blonde sex appeal was perfect for the role of Debs, as the boys liked to call her. For her role, Leslie was also able to call on her own real-life experiences sharing a home with Barbara Molyneux, one of the most beautiful and in-demand models of her era, and coping with all the male attention the two girls inevitably attracted.

It was an especially welcome piece of casting for Leslie, who was seeking to resume her career and re-establish herself after taking time out to give birth in 1990 to her first child, Joe, with her footballer husband Lee Chapman. For Leslie, *Men Behaving Badly* was to prove a spectacular comeback.

The cast duly gathered for the first rehearsals in the unlikely setting of a boys' club in Twickenham, which resembled a church hall with rows of chairs stacked up against the wall. The quartet were obliged to rehearse with the set marked out on the floor with different coloured masking tape – blue for Gary's bedroom, orange for the hallway and red for the sitting room with wooden poles outlining the doorways.

It was a primitive start, but from the off there was a discernible feeling of optimism about the project among the four principal members of the cast. They collectively laughed aloud at some of Simon Nye's writing during the read-throughs and they could all see the potential in the series from day one.

A pilot episode was filmed and Nye has admitted he thought it had gone well until he noticed that the actors looked like they had just been involved in a car crash rather than a comedy show. The writer observed in his book *The Best of Men Behaving Badly*: 'Harry Enfield was so distressed he went through his contract with a microscope, looking for a get-out clause.'

The making of each episode started with a read-through every Tuesday, followed by 'blocking' on Tuesday afternoons, in which the actors worked out their positioning and where to stand and move in relation to the camera. Wednesdays and Thursdays were taken up with more rehearsals in preparation for a full run-through on Fridays. Saturdays provided an opportunity for fine-tuning, and Sundays were taken up with a measured line-by-line rehearsal at Thames TV's studios at Teddington in Middlesex in front of the cameras and a dress rehearsal. Then, after a break in the early evening for supper, each episode was filmed before a live audience which had been expertly warmed up by comedian Ted Robbins. Frequently watching her son's performance from a seat in the audience was Martin's proud mother Daphne.

Men Behaving Badly was launched on the full ITV network on 18 February 1992, and the cast members were invited to Beryl Vertue's Tudor home in Kent to watch the first episode. They were all pleased with the result but little did they know this was the start of what would become the defining British TV comedy of the 1990s.

In the first episode viewers learned that Gary worked at a dead-end burglary alarm sales office with two old fashioned assistants, and that he and Dorothy had been together for two years. But over dinner Gary is seen suggesting they go their separate ways until he immediately thinks better of it as he can't bear the thought of not sleeping with Dorothy again. 'The minute Dorothy leaves me, I go completely to pieces,' Martin explained to one of the authors in the build up to the launch. 'But the minute she's back, I'm back ogling anything with a pulse. It *is* the male psyche.'

The chief object for such ogling turns out to be the lovely

Deborah after she introduces herself as the perky new owner of the flat upstairs. Gary and dim-wit Dermot fall over themselves in a bid to win her amorous favours. Gary goes so far as to give Deborah a gift of what he thinks is a cookbook but is in fact a book of sexual positions. His suggestion that Deborah comes down and tries out some of the ideas on him causes Dorothy to walk out.

This first episode of *Men Behaving Badly* immediately set the risqué tone that was to become so familiar and so popular with millions of viewers over the next six years. But, as the first series went on, it became clear that the show was undoubtedly suffering from being screened at 8.30pm. This was the half-hour slot before the rigidly imposed watershed, which decrees that nothing can be shown before 9pm that is too near the knuckle or which might seriously offend viewers. For a series about two young lads misbehaving, this presented very real difficulties for Simon Nye, Beryl Vertue and director Martin Dennis.

The watershed constrictions made for some lively horse-trading in the scripts between Nye and ITV's bosses – a colourful word was discarded here and there in return for the gaining of an innuendo, a risqué joke or a visual gag. However much they all hated it, compromise was the name of the game, and ultimately ITV paid the price for some thoughtless scheduling.

'In actual fact, we cut a lot out that was just too offensive,' Martin told one of the authors at the time, 'and we regret that. I also regret that because of the time slot we are not allowed to swear as much as we do, because it's accurate. I swear all the time, everybody swears all the time, but for some reason the public mustn't know that. Locker-room chat does go on, you know.'

The show opened to some heartening reviews, and the viewers began to warm to the ill-matched foursome as the first series unfolded. It largely concentrated on Martin, as Gary, struggling to break up with Dorothy while competing with Dermot for the attentions of Deborah. Subsequent episodes saw Gary persuading Dorothy to agree to an open relationship, then being consumed with jealousy when she went out with another man, and Dermot pursuing Debs in a bid to get her to sleep with him while her boyfriend was away in Singapore.

The immature boorishness of the two boys, coupled with their bloke-ish failings when it came to their attitudes towards the opposite sex, went down well with the viewers and the audience ratings at least proved encouraging for ITV. When the first series finished midway through October 1992, a second series looked to be on the cards. But, as Leslie Ash revealed in her autobiography *My Life Behaving Badly*, the all important on-screen rapport between Martin and Harry was missing.

Leslie wrote of Harry: 'There had been no real chemistry between him and Martin – it was like they were both doing one-liners, and in a sitcom you can't be too much of a solo performer, can't outshine everyone else; it needs to be a team effort.'

It was no secret that Harry hadn't particularly enjoyed doing the show, and Leslie said she was aware that there was an air about him that he was only ever going to do one series. And so it proved. Harry opted out of a second series, and Leslie had little doubt as to why. She wrote in her book: 'I think it came down to the fact that Harry was very good at doing his own material but hadn't felt at home doing someone else's. It had been obvious there was a gaping hole in the cast chemistry.'

Harry went on to prove the point when given his own BBC sketch show *Harry Enfield's Television Programme*. To general acclaim he quickly went on to develop yet more of his amusing creations, such as Tim Nice But Dim, Wayne and Waynetta Slob (with the help of Kathy Burke) and the ageing DJs Smashie and Nicey (with Paul Whitehouse). Harry looked far more comfortable and better suited to bringing his own array of characters to life in sketches rather than playing rent-dodging, skirt-chasing Dermot for six weeks in a sitcom written by someone else.

After he had quit the show, a 1950s television presenter Mr Cholmondley-Warner cropped up as a regular character in *Harry Enfield's Television Show*. And in one episode Harry gave a nod to the sitcom he had left behind when Cholmondley-Warner gazed into the future of television and envisaged a programme called *Men Behaving Splendidly*. It showed Harry had no hard feelings.

Harry's departure was seen as a bitter blow at the time. But while it came as a bombshell to Martin, Leslie and Caroline, it was no surprise whatsoever to producer Beryl

Vertue. In fact, she had been secretly fully aware that Harry was only ever going to appear in the one series. 'But I never did tell anyone,' she said. 'When he said he wouldn't do another there was shock horror everywhere, and surprise – but not for me because I knew that.'

The stark truth was that Harry's going left ITV and the rest of the *Men Behaving Badly* team in a quandary. Martin, Leslie and Caroline understandably wondered whether ITV would commission another series now the main star had gone. But Beryl was one step ahead. She had faith in the sitcom and to her re-casting Gary's flatmate was the obvious solution. 'I had to stop them all panicking that they couldn't do it,' she said. 'I pointed out that Harry played a lodger – the lodger could leave and a new one arrive.' ITV agreed and, as history has shown, the choice of Neil Morrissey proved to be inspired.

Morrissey had come to acting after a difficult childhood. He and his younger brother had been put into a children's home when the courts decided that their parents could no longer look after them. At school in his teens he had advertised on his school notice board for foster parents to help him to gain his A levels and he subsequently did well enough to go on to the Guildhall School of Music and Drama.

Neil's ambitions to become an actor had been fired by a teacher putting him in a school play. Neil often played the classroom clown at school and his teacher decided to make the most of it by handing him a decent role in the school play of *Sweeney Todd: The Demon Barber of Fleet Street*. 'I went out and got huge laughs and really enjoyed it,' he remembers.

On leaving drama school Neil gained an enviable start to his career when he landed a small part as Able Seaman Matthew Quintal in the Mel Gibson movie epic *The Bounty*. Neil's eventual breakthrough came with ITV's series *Boon*, about an invalided-out fireman running his Texas Rangers motorbike messenger company around the Midlands. Michael Elphick was the star of the show, but it brought Neil to prominence as his lovable but naïve sidekick Rocky Cassidy, a dim biker whose colourful love life found him either on the brink of passion or crying into his beer after another failed romance. His plethora of on-screen girlfriends ranged from a strippergram girl to a graffiti artist.

With his good looks and dark shoulder-length hair, and sitting astride a Norton Commando motorbike in his leathers, Neil became a heart-throb for teenage girls. Over the first three series he won himself a loyal band of female fans in the 14 to 16 age group, who wrote to him by the hundred wanting to know if he really was into heavy metal and motorbikes and whether he had a girlfriend. In fact, Neil had a wife, actress Amanda Noar, and together they had a baby son called Sam.

Neil had met Amanda in the second series of *Boon* when she had a small role as a secretary who had to chat up Rocky. Neil had fallen for her immediately and their courtship got off to the kind of start which might have come out of a *Men Behaving Badly* script. 'Our first date was at a transvestite club in Soho,' Neil revealed. 'That was Amanda's idea of a joke.'

It was Martin who suggested Neil as Harry Enfield's

replacement, and he was only too happy to recommend him from personal experience. The two actors had first met through mutual friends in a north London pub while Neil was about to make an impact in *Boon* and Martin was in *No Place Like Home*. They were living quite close to each other in north London, Neil in Crouch End and Martin in Tufnell Park, and when they got to know each other they got on like a house on fire. The friendship was sealed when Neil gave Martin a role in a film for which he was executive producer called *The Ballad of Kid Divine*. A spaghetti western spoof, the film featured Neil and Martin as two bounty hunters tracking down Kid Divine (Jesse Birdsall), a wanted killer with a baby face and a $25,000 price on his head. Martin also had a role in an episode of *Boon*, which strengthened the friendship.

Martin knew Neil would be perfect for *Men Behaving Badly*. He recognised that Neil was clearly a good actor with a lot of charm, and he already had evidence that the two of them worked well together. They enjoyed a matey rapport which the show called for, and he was confident they could project this bond on screen. Moreover, Neil looked very different from Martin, which was a bonus.

So, with Martin's enthusiastic backing, Neil met up with Beryl Vertue for an exploratory lunch and impressed her enough to be asked to step straight into Harry Enfield's shoes. He did so with relish.

Neil's arrival as Tony proved a real fillip for the cast because it was clear to everyone that he and Martin hit it off from the very start. To make the newcomer feel at home, a party was thrown to welcome Neil, who was most appreciative of the gesture. It turned into a raucous jolly at the bar of Thames TV's studios at Teddington which stretched noisily into the small hours before everyone staggered off home. It was an enjoyable start to what was to become a great screen partnership.

As she watched the two actors start working together, Leslie Ash was relieved and delighted to detect real chemistry between the two male leads. 'It was like electricity between the two of them,' she recalled. 'Martin began to change Gary from the Yuppie-type suit of series one to the slightly shambolic guy who became a comic icon. Without Harry it became a show about four characters.'

Leslie reflected: 'No disrespect, but series one had felt a bit like the Harry Enfield Show – he was the big star and *MBB* was about Dermot and three people in his life. Now it was suddenly about four characters and better for it.'

Somewhat unusually, ITV accorded *Men Behaving Badly* a rapid turnaround in the schedules, allowing the second series to reach the screen barely five months after the first had finished. The opening episode of series two was saddled with the potentially tricky task of explaining to viewers that Harry Enfield, the big star of the show, had gone. But a surprisingly smooth transition was effected with Martin, as Gary, explaining Harry's absence by revealing he had received a postcard from Dermot saying he had fallen in love with a croupier and wouldn't be back because he was going around the world on her Yamaha motorbike.

This allowed Martin to advertise for a new flatmate and

eventually settle upon Neil as record seller Tony Smart after being distinctly underwhelmed by the other prospective lodgers. So free of problems was Morrissey's integration into the show that Dermot was never mentioned again until the fifth series when viewers learned he had taken a job testing the rides at EuroDisney.

For the viewers, Tony proved to be a very different character from Dermot. The only similarity between the two was that once Tony had set eyes on Deborah he too was equally determined to get her into his bed. But unlike Gary, Tony was fanciable and could be a success with girls, which would give the show a whole new dimension.

From the start, Neil looked to be a much better fit than Harry. Once Gary had chosen Tony as his new flatmate, he established himself so quickly that it was easy to forget that Dermot had ever existed. Leslie Ash was not alone in noticing that Neil's overall impact was immediate: 'The chemistry the four developed off-screen translated well on to the screen. *MBB* had changed instantly for the better when Neil had arrived. With his long dark hair and slim good looks, Neil brought an important new element to the show.'

On screen the show appeared to be going from strength to strength, and Martin and the rest of the team were heartened to win Best ITV Sitcom at the 1992 British Comedy Awards. But behind the scenes during the second series there was a growing anxiety and a noticeable insecurity among cameramen, make-up girls and other production staff as they went about their work.

The reason for the palpable display of nerves was the rumour mill ominously whispering that Thames TV could be in danger of losing their franchise and with it their licence to broadcast. That would almost inevitably mean the end of *Men Behaving Badly*. By the time shooting of the second series was nearing its end, an atmosphere of real fear was pervading the entire production.

The second series went out on ITV early in September 1992 and finished its run on 13 October. Thanks in no small way to the introduction of Neil, it was a much better show than the first, but disappointingly for all concerned, audience figures were down, almost certainly because Harry Enfield's fans had departed with him. The show was also increasingly handicapped by its pre-watershed scheduling. As everyone involved with the series could see only too well, it desperately needed to be screened in a later slot.

'Within two series we'd quickly exhausted the possibilities where you could say "Golly!" in a programme called *Men Behaving Badly*,' said Martin. 'We needed to cover the territory that the title suggested a bit more.' ITV's schedulers, however, seemed intent on preserving the post-9pm slot for its drama output.

Not long afterwards, Beryl Vertue telephoned the cast to tell them the grim news – Thames TV had indeed lost its licence. It would cease broadcasting at the end of the year and *Men Behaving Badly* was to be cancelled. Beryl had gone off to New Zealand for a long and expensive holiday fully believing the show would be re-commissioned, so it came as a profound shock to her that ITV had decided not to take up its option for a third series in the wake of Thames TV's lost franchise.

The cancellation was all the more disappointing for her because she knew just how good *Men Behaving Badly* was – and that it could be even better. 'That made me rather cross,' she said later with understatement. Beryl knew it was a huge mistake to cancel the show, and the viewing public seemed to agree with her when they voted *Men Behaving Badly* the Most Popular Comedy Series at the 1993 National Television Awards.

Beryl stressed to all involved with *Men Behaving Badly* that the cancellation did not signal the end of the programme by any means. Gamely she told Martin and the other cast members that she was determined to work hard and fight to get the show back on TV somehow. Martin could not help but admire Beryl for her tenacity and her unshakeable faith in the show, but at that moment the odds looked stacked against its return. Beryl planned to pitch it to the BBC, but it was almost unheard of for a programme to transfer from a commercial channel to the BBC.

The axing of the show was a bitter disappointment for Martin. Like Neil, Leslie and Caroline, he believed *Men Behaving Badly* was a winner and the four of them were growing into their roles with increasing assurance. 'It was a horrible time when ITV said they wouldn't re-commission it,' Leslie said. 'We just went, "Why?" We couldn't understand it.' Despite Beryl's bold fighting talk, they held out no great hopes for the show's swift return and had no option but to seek work elsewhere.

Martin might not be every woman's idea of the sexiest man in the world, but he turned out to be high on the list when it came to having a laugh about sex. As the new ITV company Carlton launched itself in 1993, the show that hit most of the headlines was *The Good Sex Guide*. Liverpudlian actress Margi Clarke presented the show that provoked delight and derision, and Martin, who somehow managed to convey naughtiness and innocence at the same time, was the most amusing star of the many saucy sketches.

Martin went on to feature heavily in a 1995 follow-up series called *Jeremy Hardy Gives Good Sex*, in which he memorably played a penis called Private Parts. The routines won no prizes for subtlety as Private Parts was questioned by his commanding officer: 'Tell me, Private, exactly how long is it since you've seen active service?'

There was a great deal of controversy attached to the *Good Sex* shows, and the story about the disappearance of the famous British reserve went around the world. But Martin could not see what all the fuss was about. 'Some of the writing was very funny, and there were some genuinely hilarious moments,' he said. 'There is a funny side to the whole subject of sex. We didn't understand the disapproval at all.'

CHAPTER 5

MARRIAGE BREAK-UP

*'I didn't want to be Lucy Clunes any more.
I wanted to be Lucy Aston'*
MARTIN'S FIRST WIFE LUCY ON THE BREAK UP
OF THEIR MARRIAGE

The cancellation of *Men Behaving Badly* could hardly have come at a worse time for Martin. His marriage to Lucy had run into difficulties and by now it was failing to the extent that they were considering splitting up.

In the time they had been married, their fortunes as actors had changed drastically. Martin was fast climbing the ladder of success with decent roles in a variety of projects, including two series of ITV's *Gone to the Dogs,* two series of *Men Behaving Badly* and a role in the Disney film *Swing Kids* with glamorous Hollywood actress Barbara Hershey, which saw him spending time filming in Prague.

With success came a new confidence about Martin. It was onwards and upwards for the young actor, and he and his wife were determined to enjoy their success. They ate out frequently, drank copiously and enjoyed socialising. Their parties were the talk of their friends, and Martin was the life and soul of the party with his hilarious impressions of John Travolta's moves in *Saturday Night Fever*.

Lucy, meanwhile, had a semi-regular part in *Waiting for God*, a sitcom about two spirited residents of a retirement home who run rings around the management and their own families. But her priorities in life were changing, and she was beginning to tire of the partying. 'It was very superficial and I wanted more out of life,' she was quoted as saying. 'I went through a sort of crisis and got very depressed.' As well as her acting stints, Lucy was also working in a health food shop for £3.50 an hour and was making voluntary visits to Moorfields eye hospital to offer her services with talking books. Later she began to train as a crisis counsellor.

At this point, Martin and Neil were not yet the iconic television stars they were to become. But as buddies, the two young men were becoming as tight as two firm friends could be, and it led to some hard partying and life in the fast lane from which Lucy was either excluded or chose not to join in.

At times Martin's indulgences in the excesses of a showbiz lifestyle resulted in him coming home much the worse for wear in the wee small hours, or sometimes not at all, while Lucy fretted at home, ringing friends to try to discover her husband's whereabouts. 'When we met, we were both party animals,' she stressed. 'We wanted the same things in life – but then I changed, I wanted more out of life, but he thought I'd become dull and boring.'

Their contrasting lifestyles and needs inevitably led to escalating rows. Martin has carefully avoided speaking about the difficulties within the marriage or why it eventually had to come to an end. But when, long after they had split up, he described the marriage as 'rotten', Lucy was stung into a reply in the newspapers.

Lucy's version of the straw that broke the camel's back was when the couple were out to dinner at their favourite Chinese restaurant and a blazing row blew up over a party Martin had attended the night before without either telling her or choosing to invite her along.

Furious, she felt she had had enough. She said she took off her wedding ring, slammed it down on the table and stormed out, before jumping into her car and driving to Alexandra Palace where she calmly smoked a cigarette and looked at the view. It was 4 July, she noted, and thought to herself that, fittingly, this was her own personal Independence Day as well as that of America. When the couple met up again back at the flat, they both agreed it would be best to part and vowed to stay friends. That night Martin went off to stay at a friend's place.

In a bid to clear her head and get over the depressing situation, Lucy flew off to America to take a three-month holiday with members of her family. When she returned to London, she met up with Martin at one of their favourite restaurants, Le Pont de la Tour, on the Thames, but reconciliation proved impossible. It was evident that they could no longer go on living together.

While Lucy returned to the flat, Martin had moved out to live with friends. It was a confusing and worrying time for him, and he led a somewhat nomadic existence courtesy of friends who variously took him in and gave him refuge for a period of six months while he sorted out his future.

It wasn't until Martin set about finding somewhere at least semi-permanent to live on his own that it was brought home to him that a chapter in his life had now closed irrevocably. His marriage to Lucy was over and there was no going back.

Resignedly he started looking for a flat to rent, eventually taking a look at a two-bedroom flat on the fourth floor of an unprepossessing, six-storey, red brick block at Queen's Quay in Queenhithe, on the north side of the Thames near Southwark Bridge. Queenhithe is steeped in history: as well as being one of the earliest post-Roman docks in the City of London, it was here that Queen Matilda established London's first public lavatory.

The builders of the Queen's Quay block had originally planned to erect a hotel, but the plans evolved into a building that would contain offices and a number of flats. The unfriendly-looking block certainly wasn't to everyone's taste, but when Martin walked along the corridor and entered number 419 for the first time he was taken by its great redeeming feature: it offered fine views of the river and beyond. It had communal access to the roof with even better views stretching from Tower Bridge to Waterloo Bridge. He knew he could do a lot worse than live there.

The flat had previously been home to students and on first inspection was none too appealing to Martin. While the students' style of living mercifully fell short of Gary's and

Tony's squalid pad in *Men Behaving Badly*, it was not exactly 'des res' and the décor left a lot to be desired. But at least it was centrally located – Martin later discovered that he could walk into town without much difficulty – and it offered an ever-changing view of diverse river traffic.

Importantly, with a divorce now looming, Martin knew it was just about affordable at £100 a week, and he decided to move in. He took time to get settled and make it a home, but at least it was a base from which he could rebuild his life. It would be a new start.

While Martin was finding his feet again, Beryl Vertue was showing her mettle in the TV circles that mattered and was refusing to let *Men Behaving Badly* die. True to her promise to Martin and the others, she says she did 'the only logical thing' and got in touch with Alan Yentob, a top boss at the BBC. She later explained: 'If you are going to do something no one has done before – move a cancelled series from one network to another – then you have to go to the top person. You cannot go further down with a big decision and expect it to be pushed up for you,' she reasoned. 'Their jobs could be at risk. I just kept saying that I knew it would work.'

Beryl argued passionately that she had great belief in *Men Behaving Badly* and that the BBC could have a hit on its hands if it picked up the show and gave it room to fly by screening it in a later slot.

Yentob admits he didn't really have any hesitation about taking *Men Behaving Badly*. 'Let's be clear,' he said, 'taking a show from ITV is one thing, but to take a show from ITV and repeat it on BBC 1, that was weird. No one had ever done that before. I did it for the very simple reason that I loved the show. I thought it was great, and ITV having something good but not realising its potential was appealing.'

It took time, but by 1994 Beryl was able to ring Martin, Leslie, Neil and Caroline with the good news that the BBC had commissioned a new series of *Men Behaving Badly*. 'I told you I'd get it back on the screen,' she told Martin triumphantly. It was a joyous and welcome surprise, and he couldn't help but admire Beryl's tenacity. The show was indeed back on and crucially, all four principals were available and eager to pick up where they had left off.

Thus it was with a renewed sense of optimism and no little excitement that the quartet were joyfully reunited at the BBC's rehearsal rooms in Kensington to prepare for the new series, to be screened in the summer of 1994.

It was at once apparent from the scripts that Simon Nye would enjoy greater licence in his writing from the BBC bosses than he had previously been granted by ITV. The BBC plan for the new series was to schedule it in the post-watershed slot of 9.30pm. Now the language could be more colourful and the subject matter more adult, especially when it came to the topic of sex.

The first episode was a case in point. Gary was seen to be feeling sexually inferior to Tony when the subject came up of how many women the pair had each slept with. Gary exaggerated but then set out to provide proof of his numerous conquests to an unconvinced Dorothy and Tony.

Dorothy memorably decided that Gary's ideal woman would be 'a top-heavy 18-year-old aerobics instructor who owned an off-licence'.

The switch from ITV to BBC was undoubtedly a blessing for Nye's writing. As well as post-watershed freedom, it afforded him an important extra five minutes per episode in which to develop his characters – time gained each week because of the absence of commercials.

A Friday night in July, however, was hardly the ideal slot for a relaunch of *Men Behaving Badly*, but the series did surprisingly well for a summer schedule filler. It ended with something of a teaser for the viewers with a none-too-sober Gary proposing to Dorothy and regretting it the next morning. When the third series was given a repeat, it was astutely scheduled right after *Absolutely Fabulous*. It meant that *Men Behaving Badly* thus inherited a sizeable audience already enjoying a good laugh – and the show was strong enough to retain that audience and build upon it.

'That led to our fourth series which I think was the best and the funniest,' Martin said. 'Then it went bonkers. The publicity machine went mental, and we were asked for comments on serious matters of the day!' In time, *Men Behaving Badly* would replace *Absolutely Fabulous* as the nation's favourite comedy.

In countless interviews Martin was asked if he shared any of the laddish traits his character Gary displayed. He was at pains to point out that he was a married man and nothing like Gary, although he happily confessed that there had certainly been a bit of the lad in him for as long as he could remember. Yes, he said, he had indeed shared a flat with other guys and there had indeed been hi-jinks.

'And yes,' Martin confided, 'I've behaved badly towards women. Mind you,' he quickly added, 'I've been shat upon by women myself.'

Recalling his skirt-chasing teens and early twenties, he said: 'I do actually remember once waking up next to a girl I'd met the night before in a room I'd never seen before in my life, and when she went out to make some tea I was searching around her room to find something with her name written on it because I didn't know her name – which is awful, awful. And all for what? But when you are young, consequences don't come into it, do they?

'I don't know where it comes from, but there's that need for guys to make some kind of conquest in their teens and early twenties. But as you get older, the awful feeling in the morning after a one-night stand stays in your memory.

'When I left school at 16 and went to the Arts Educational school, they had a drama department, a musical department and a dance department and I turned up there at 16 to be confronted by these young girls wandering around in what looked like swimming costumes. It was a good six months before I could stand up without embarrassment!

'Naturally I fell in love left right and centre, but at that age you can't separate wanting to sleep with girls from being in love with them. So you kinda think, "My God, this girl is really attractive. I love her." But you don't love her – you just want to bed her. So, sure, I got my heart broken, but when you look around for the next girl, you get a name as a Casanova when in fact you're not – you've been dumped, and you've just got to fill that space. It's all unfair!'

Martin said he had fond memories of his own flat-sharing days after he had left drama school. 'That was mayhem!' he grinned. 'They were crazy times – we all had mad hours.' He shared a flat with a friend called Iain in Putney, in south west London, and he took a job washing up in a local restaurant until his pal started training to be a chef and landed a job at the Great American Disaster. This was a trendy eaterie situated at the smarter end of the Fulham Road, and before long Martin found himself also working there as a chef at the recommendation of Iain's brother Clive. 'He got me a job there until I got the sack for being seven hours late because I was doing a double shift,' Martin recounted ruefully.

Martin subsequently landed a job preparing vegetables at L'Escargot, a prestigious restaurant in Greek Street in Soho in the heart of London's West End. 'I topped and tailed the vegetables, but I was allowed to make steak tartare,' he said proudly. 'I learned a great deal there – and you see more prima donna behaviour there than in any theatre I've ever seen!'

Once his shift was over at L'Escargot, Martin would head for the Zanzibar, then just about the smartest cocktail bar in London, where Iain was now working. The night was still young and there were girls, drinks and good times to be enjoyed. But, said Martin, when it came to competing for the favours of the opposite sex, his flatmates won hands down. 'It was always a big shock to all of us if I ever got a girl,' he laughed, 'because they were both better looking than I was. We never fell out about girls, though. There was only bitter resentment on my part because I was getting no action – rather like Gary.'

While *Men Behaving Badly* cannot claim the sole credit for spawning the cult of laddism, the series certainly arrived right on cue. The timing could not have been better, coinciding as it did with a surge in politically incorrect humour from the likes of comedian Frank Skinner, and with the wild lifestyles, fierce fraternal disputes and couldn't-care-less attitudes of Liam and Noel Gallagher, who had shot to notoriety in the rock band Oasis. The title of the TV series quickly entered into common usage and provided tabloid editors with a topical headline to describe any wayward antics of politicians, celebrities and footballers. Foremost among them at the time was England soccer star Paul Gascoigne, who regularly hit the front pages while out on drinking sprees with celebrity pals like Chris Evans and Danny Baker.

On TV, Frank Skinner expanded the laddism theme by revelling in football fantasies with David Baddiel. Britain's young lads had always enjoyed booze, birds and football, not necessarily in that order, but now it seemed there was no shame whatsoever in admitting it – especially in the pages of the ultimate lads' mag *Loaded*. This was launched in 1994 with a masthead reading 'For men who should know better' and it hit the newsagents just as *Men Behaving Badly* was really taking off.

With each episode, Nye's scripts had Martin and Neil steadily building upon Gary's and Tony's TV identities with a catalogue of misbehaviour. They emerged as lager-swilling, flatulent, Baywatch-ogling, Kylie-fixated lads who were obsessed with female breasts, or 'shirt potatoes' as they were described in one episode. The lads had a fridge stocked with nothing but lager and the mouldy remains of a take-away curry, and they lived like slobs.

The two girls proved the perfect foil, just about putting up with the mayhem while pointing out the absurd childishness of the boys' behaviour. The girls were strong, while the boys were weak. While Gary struggled to maintain a grown-up relationship with Dorothy, Tony went to ever more desperate efforts to impress Deborah, even going so far as to offer to shave his pubic hair for charity. Martin said of Gary and Tony: 'In a sense they're struggling to grow up. But they're struggling not to grow up.'

It wasn't long before Martin's portrayal of Gary was seized upon by the media as a lads' icon and he was soon featured on the front cover of *Loaded* with a headline proclaiming 'Martin Clunes is... GOLDENBALLS'. Martin beamed out from an issue which offered, in addition to the obligatory pictures of scantily clad girls, the legendary boozer 'Ollie Reed's cocktail guide', a feature on 'drinking around the Monopoly board' and a 'massive bacon sarnie poster'.

These low-brow topics might just as well have come straight from one of Gary's and Tony's lager-fuelled late-night discussions about the female anatomy, the mysteries of the opposite sex and the naming of 'the top five arses of female singers' – Kylie was the winning name they chorused together instantly. Simon Nye felt dialogue between men was a separate language and he captured it perfectly.

Birds, boobs, and booze – with intermittent burps – tended to be the subjects that dominated Gary and Tony's philosophical conversations on their pizza-stained sofa. Their musings included 'how wonderful it would be to have breasts but what a responsibility' and 'how do reindeer with large antlers bend down to tie their hooflaces.' This was the kind of comedy *Loaded* readers lapped up eagerly.

It was Martin's misfortune to enhance his on-screen image when he was banned for a year and fined £350 after admitting a drink-driving offence. After stopping to buy cigarettes one morning in the early hours, he had forgotten to turn on the lights of his grey BMW and he was spotted by police in Bloomsbury and given a breath test. When the case came to court, barrister Andrew Lewis said on his behalf: 'This is very much an example of carelessness rather than taking a chance. Mr Clunes had had some beer with a friend but was careful not to drink more than would put him over the limit. He did not take into account he had had something to drink at lunchtime as well.'

Asked after the case if he was behaving badly, Martin replied: 'Yes, of course I was. This is one of the country's better laws and I broke it. So I am being punished.' Losing his licence was an inconvenience for Martin, but with touching loyalty, Neil went out of his way to give Martin lifts in his own car until he regained his licence.

With a hint of admiration, *Loaded* later noted the cool Martin had mustered to open a beer festival three days after getting done for drink driving.

However, Tim Southwell, one of the founders of *Loaded*, explained in his book *Getting Away With It (The Inside Story of Loaded)* that it had never been the magazine's intention to replace New Man with New Lad. *Loaded*'s message, he wrote, was: 'Don't take us too seriously, we're blokes and we're useless... We like football, but that doesn't mean we're hooligans... We like looking at pictures of fancy ladies sometimes but that doesn't mean we want to rape them.' The description could just as easily have fitted Gary and Tony.

Beryl Vertue, however, expressed surprise that *Men Behaving Badly* was continually being credited with the birth of laddism. 'When you start a new series, you do it because you believe in it,' she stressed, 'and because it makes you laugh. That's what I thought about this, thought it was different. It made me laugh but it turned out in the end to be something much bigger and it took me by surprise that we were apparently the beginning of laddism.'

She went on to say in the *Independent*: 'Outrageous though we are, one of the things that accounts for our success is that it's a very truthful show. People don't like to admit how truthful it is, but so many times you hear people say: "They're just like my boyfriend or husband." That's why people aren't offended by it. You'd imagine that this is a show

77

which women wouldn't like because it's so chauvinistic. But women love Gary and Tony because they are very innocent. They're like little boys; not vindictive in any way.'

Neil backed up Beryl's view of Gary and Tony. 'They're just a couple of sad gits,' he declared. 'One of them doesn't work and one of them is a security consultant. People seem to think that in the series we're burping, farting, womanising, shagging, football hooligans which is absolutely, completely and utterly wrong. The characters are feeble, inadequate, pathetic, never-go-to-bed-with-anyone, halitosis-infected gits. But their redeeming qualities are a natural charm and vulnerability.'

When assessing the show's extraordinary success and massive following, Martin said: 'It was down to timing as much as the content of the programme, the sort of social revolutions, or whatever, that go on. I think there'd been a backlash to the feminist sort of berating of men for all the problems of the world.'

As Martin shrewdly pointed out, *Men Behaving Badly*'s buddy-buddy area was one which had not been covered in British television comedy since *The Likely Lads*. 'And a lot has changed since then,' he said.

But there certainly were similarities: *The Likely Lads*, which was first launched in 1964, followed the escapades and romantic pursuits of a cocky, cynical jack the lad called Terry, played by James Bolam, and his shyer but more ambitious drinking partner Bob, played by Rodney Bewes.

Like *Men Behaving Badly*, the 1960s sitcom was a massive hit, appreciated by men and women equally. It garnered a faithful following until it finished in 1969 before returning in 1973 with an even better series called *Whatever Happened To The Likely Lads?* in which the boys, after playing the field, learned to their chagrin that women sometimes like to change men and control them. Either for authenticity or for sheer joy, the Likely Lads drank real beer on the show, and in one episode Bewes estimated that he got through nine pints of bitter – something which Gary and Tony would have admired.

Simon Nye felt his two creations were mainly gormless and actually quite gentle. They were not given to doing unpleasant things to their mates or girlfriends, he stressed. The constraints of being a BBC comedy meant that the grossest excesses of male behaviour could never be served up to *Men Behaving Badly*'s audience. Although the boys were portrayed as consumers of considerable amounts of alcohol, the dangers of excessive drinking was made clear as Gary and Tony nursed painful hangovers, behaved erratically and tended to speak incoherent nonsense after an alcoholic binge. 'No one is holding either of the characters up as role models,' Martin frequently pointed out. 'It's very clear they are utter shits. In fact, I feel rather sorry for my character Gary.'

CHAPTER 6

HOUSEHOLD NAMES

'It was fantastic and it turned my career around'
MARTIN CLUNES LOOKING BACK ON THE
SUCCESS OF MEN BEHAVING BADLY

The success of *Men Behaving Badly* was reflected in its soaring ratings. Its fourth series was regularly watched by more than 10 million viewers, rising at its peak to around 17 million, the show turned Martin into one of the most popular – and most recognisable – stars on British television. While Neil garnered the saucy mail from female fans, Martin won the more mature female following, who saw Gary as a fairly harmless lad who simply needed some motherly guidance to grow up. Fans of Neil wanted a date, while Martin's fans tended to ask for an autograph. And as they went about their daily lives, neither Martin nor Neil was ever short of male followers of the series giving them a slap on the back and offering to buy them a pint.

The extraordinary impact of the show upon the public was brought home to Neil and Caroline following the screening of the episode in which Tony and Dorothy went to bed together while Gary and Deborah were away on a writing course. 'You shouldn't have done it!' was the scolding each of them received when they were spotted out and about leading their own individual off-screen lives.

Martin and Neil were each paid a reputed £15,000 per show when the programme was at its peak in 1996. Leslie and Caroline had reportedly been paid £25,000 less per series than the boys and they were understandably none too happy about it. But the two actresses managed to secure a similar fee for themselves after holding out for parity with the boys – a pay hike for the girls which happily had the backing of the boys.

Caroline also held out for more jokes and funny lines for the girls, believing that the women in the show were the butt of too many jokes. She said she felt Dorothy was portrayed as 'some harridan nurse and Deborah was just some totty upstairs and there was no irony in that.' Caroline's observation produced a suitable response from Simon Nye.

The high profile of each member of the *Men Behaving Badly* cast saw them flooded with offers for commercials and various endorsements, both individually and collectively. And when they all appeared together in an advertisement for a clothing firm owned by Cartier, not only were they handsomely paid but they were also given beautiful and hugely expensive watches.

Martin, it transpired, was the most marketable of the four. Leslie noted in her autobiography: 'Martin was the most in demand and, in the days before mobile phones, he had a pager that used to keep beeping in rehearsals. As he rushed off to the pay phone to call his agent about yet another job, we'd all shout "Kerrrrrrrching!"'

To his credit, Martin turned down more offers of commercials than he took. He chose judiciously, turning down the huge sum of £650,000 to appear in a beer commercial. But in 1995 he appeared with Caroline Quentin in an advert for Pizza Hut's Stuffed Crust. The ad featured Martin ogling stunning model Paula Abbott until Caroline gets her revenge by shoving the pizza into his drooling mouth.

Later he was paid a reputed £500,000 for his part in a multi-million pound advertising campaign for Nescafé. In a clever reversal of his *Men Behaving Badly* image, the amusing advert showed Martin hammering on the door of his noisy young neighbours, objecting to the racket as they hold rehearsals for their rock band. Angrily he asks: 'Do you know what time it is?' Back comes the reply: 'No – is it by the Stones?' The lead singer then attempts to calm things down with mugs of coffee – and Martin returns clutching a recorder in the hope of joining the band.

All four stars of *Men Behaving Badly* fared well and lucratively away from the show. Individually they were a big draw, but the thought of Martin and Neil teaming up to plug products aimed at men had the advertising industry more than willing to reach for their cheque books. Very wisely the pair steered clear of becoming a double act but teamed up occasionally, notably for a 1997 ad for Honda's CR-V four-wheel-drive car. The advert featured the boys showing off the car in an effort to attract a glamorous woman.

Martin's extraordinary laddish TV persona proved so popular that it even saw him appear on the front cover of *Sunday* magazine, sitting in a chair naked save for a pair of black Chelsea boots. A sideways-on pose preserved his modesty.

The show proved to be a remarkable ratings success for the BBC, much to the chagrin of the ITV bosses, whose judgement in letting the series go had proved to be so poor. The BBC bosses were naturally jubilant. Not only were they rubbing the noses of the rival channel in the mire but they were proving yet again that when it came to situation comedy the BBC was streets ahead.

Interestingly, research showed that more than half the viewers tuning in each week turned out to be women – which further rubbed salt into ITV's wounds when the potential for advertisers was taken into account. The findings showed that women enjoyed seeing Dorothy and Deborah coming out on top. They were much brighter, sharper and brainier than the boys, who were just harmless chumps, and the series seemed to confirm that all men were just kids at heart.

Meanwhile, *Men Behaving Badly*'s male following appreciated the bond between the two buddies, who happily sent each other up but were essentially supportive of each other. Male fans also recognised Gary and Tony's dilemma as the best of buddies: do they love their mate more than their girlfriend? And the series had that priceless theme of unrequited love from afar in the relationship between Tony and Deborah.

In 1995, Martin was gratified to win Top Television Comedy Actor in the British Comedy Awards. The following year he gained further recognition by winning a BAFTA award for Top Comedy Performance. The show itself also won a clutch of awards, including Best Situation Comedy at the 1996 Royal Television Society Awards, beating Channel 4's *Father Ted* and the BBC's *Absolutely Fabulous*. The judges praised *Men Behaving Badly* for being 'truthful and funny'. In celebration, Martin and Neil couldn't pass up the chance of a little Gary-Tony slice of impish misbehaviour. With the help of a pen-sized laser, they were able to direct a dancing blob of red light on to the faces of a group of dinner-jacketed TV executives sitting at the next table after their meal.

In addition to the awards, Martin was particularly gratified by the acclaim from the critics, and not just from the tabloids that had been quick to treat Gary and Tony as favoured naughty sons. The *Guardian* said of *Men Behaving Badly*: 'It has tapped into the zeitgeist and has won a ridiculous number of awards. It has become a national institution.'

'A wonderful script and wonderful performances,' said the *Daily Mirror*. 'It's all very funny, very watchable, one of the best things currently on TV.' And the *Daily Express* declared: 'So good that the BBC schedule could hardly live without it.' London's *Evening Standard* decided the show was 'near perfect', *The Times* praised it as 'undeniably funny' and the *People* declared it to be 'disgraceful and hilarious'.

But *Men Behaving Badly* was not to everyone's liking. There were accusations that the show was a glaring example of dumbing down Britain and of TV in general. Conservative MP Sir Patrick Cormack denounced it as loutish and unedifying. While campaigning for a reduction in violence and antisocial behaviour on television, he said: 'It portrays people almost as heroes who are the very opposite of that. The characters are conducting their lives in a way that no child should admire.'

As it was a comedy, however, *Men Behaving Badly* fell well short of relying on really repugnant male misbehaviour or illegal antics for its laughs, although Martin and Neil often pressed for the boundaries to be stretched. The possibility of the lads taking drugs, for example, was ruled out. 'That's regarded as dangerous territory,' Martin was quoted as saying at the time. He was keen, however, to 'keep it ugly'.

Inevitably there were some complaints from viewers, but in 1996 the Broadcasting Standards Council cleared the show of being gratuitous and unfunny. However, it did decide that *Men Behaving Badly* had 'come very close to the limit of acceptability.'

Skilfully, Simon Nye continued to move the show forward without overstepping the bounds of decency, though he came close on more than one occasion. Tony was given a succession of girlfriends before finally persuading Deborah to sleep with him in series six. Dorothy was then scripted to

Martin with Harry Enfield –
is original partner in
Men Behaving Badly.

Above left: The *Men Behaving Badly* cast we all came to love – Martin Clunes, Neil Morrissey, Caroline Quentin and Leslie Ash.

Above right: Martin at his wedding to Philippa Braithwaite in 1997.

Below: 'Gary and Tony' play up to their laddish image while promoting a Macmillan Cancer Relief event.

bove left: Martin with Neil Morrissey at the 1999 British Comedy Awards.

bove right: Promoting *Hunting Venus*, in which Martin played 80s rock star
imon Delancey.

elow left: Martin appearing alongside Paul Merton in *Aladdin*, ITV's pantomime
a 2000.

elow right: Dogs have always been a big part of Martin's life and are a never-
iding source of entertainment!

Martin pictured in 2001.
During that year he played
Captain Stickles in the
BBC's adaptation of
Lorna Doone.

Above: Martin as serial killer John Haigh in *A is for Acid*.

Below: On the set of feature-length comedy drama *The Booze Cruise* in 2002.

Above left: Martin with wife Philippa at the 2003 TV Quick Awards.

Above right: Reunited with Caroline Quentin for *Trapped* in 2004, which also starred Richard Wilson.

Below left and right: Martin as undertaker William Shawcross (*left*) and with *William and Mary* co-star Julie Graham.

bove left: At the 2004 British Comedy Awards, where *Doc Martin* won Best TV
omedy Drama.

bove right: An uncharacteristic smile from Doc Martin, on set in Port Isaac,
ornwall.

elow: Martin appearing on *Parkinson* in 2005, alongside Stephen Fry.

Martin with his dog, Tina, on *The Paul O'Grady Show* in October 2005.

take the opportunity to move in with Gary while Tony was conveniently away.

Martin revealed that he saw Gary's and Dorothy's live-in consummation of their relationship as a chance to suggest she could become pregnant followed by a 'who's the father?' mystery that could run through the fifth series. Martin's idea was that the whodunnit would culminate in Dorothy giving birth to an Asian baby. It was a funny idea for a storyline but not one which made it on to the screen.

One idea which did work well, however, was a guest appearance by singer Kylie Minogue in a sequence specially filmed for Comic Relief in 1997. Kylie, for so long an object of the boys' lustful adoration from afar, showed up at their flat wanting to use their telephone after becoming involved in an accident in her car outside. But, in a clever twist, neither Gary nor Tony recognised their fantasy girl suddenly made flesh in their midst. It was not until after she had thanked them and left that it dawned on them it was Kylie.

Prior to filming this sequence, Martin and Neil were both genuinely excited at the prospect of meeting and working with Kylie. As a jape, Martin sent Neil a fax purporting to be from the Aussie singer saying how she had a big crush on Martin and how difficult it must be for Neil, the ugly one of the duo, to be working alongside such a good-looking actor as Martin Clunes. Neil had his suspicions it was Martin pulling his leg, but he also had enough doubt to check it out with Martin!

Another inspired piece of casting proved to be Liz Carling in a cameo role. Liz just happened to be Neil's long-standing girlfriend. She and Neil had fallen in love while appearing together in *Boon*, and now she was given the role of a girl who ended up in Gary's bed as a one-night stand.

Liz played Carol, one of two girls whom Gary invited to join his barbecue after spotting them in skimpy shorts and bikini tops in the garden of the house next door. Although Liz was a beautiful young woman, she was cast against type with the script calling for her to be a bit of a frump in owlish glasses. Gary thinks he's drawn the short straw when Carol takes an interest in him, but she unexpectedly reveals herself to be as eager for sex as he is.

Liz had known Martin well for many years through Neil, and she thought it very strange to find herself kissing him passionately for the camera in front of her real-life boyfriend. 'Stop him! He's kissing my bird!' was the cry that went up from a giggling Neil during rehearsals.

While moving forward the relationships of the four principal characters, Simon Nye also pushed the boundaries of bad taste. But he was clever enough to ensure that the ruder the lines, the funnier they were – which minimised offence. He got away with Gary's problems in the trouser department by alluding to 'Mr Toad curled up asleep in Toad Hall'. The show's director Martin Dennis reflected: 'I'm sure a huge proportion of the audience were tuning in to see something more smutty than they'd ever seen on television before. You can't get away from it – people like a bit of smut.'

As the writer, Nye was also not averse to finding a laugh from a line drawing attention to Martin's prominent ears. One episode contained the observation that Gary's ears were like the handles of the FA Cup. In another, Nye had Dorothy's new boyfriend Jamie declaring it must be a relief for her now to be going out with a man whose ears didn't 'look like they were welded on by a drunk Albanian'. Martin took it all in good heart.

In 1998, the BBC chose to make *Men Behaving Badly* the centrepiece of its Christmas schedule, an accolade previously accorded to *Only Fools and Horses* and, in earlier years, to *Morecambe and Wise*. Viewers were treated to a festive package of three special programmes over the holiday period. They became the most watched programmes of the week, but the show managed to go out on a wave of controversy with a distinctly below-the-belt gag about masturbation and a sticky tissue which ends up stuck to Dorothy's head. This particular episode was screened at a time on Christmas Day when, despite the watershed, youngsters and grannies were most likely gathered in front of the TV as part of the family's seasonal festivities.

Simon Nye had considered the subject of masturbation to be fair game in a series about two lusty young lads living on their own and at the time of writing this particular episode he had no idea it would be screened on Christmas Day. 'I think it was a mistake to put it out on Christmas Day,' he later remarked in *Comedy Connections*, a TV programme looking back at *Men Behaving Badly*'s roots.

The Christmas trilogy of 45-minute episodes signalled the end of *Men Behaving Badly*, finishing with Dorothy managing to give birth at home, despite Gary stumbling in drunk and accidentally knocking out the midwife. The baby turned out to be a girl who, unbeknown to Dorothy, Gary had decided to name Kylie.

On the final day of filming the four stars felt there might be a few tears of emotion, either by themselves or the audience. But the overriding feeling among Martin, Neil, Caroline and Leslie was one of relief. They had known for weeks that the end was nigh and they all felt they had done themselves and the show full justice. Now they were laying it to rest and quitting while they were ahead.

Beryl Vertue likes to stress that it was the team's collective choice to end the series. She says Simon Nye had simply reached a point where he wasn't sure what else he could write about the boys and girls as they were. 'So we thought we'd end while we were doing wonderfully and leaving people sad that we'd gone,' she said.

'It got around that I loathed *Men Behaving Badly* by the seventh series, but that's so untrue,' Martin once said. 'I am very grateful to it and all it brought me.

'It was fantastic and totally turned my career around, but all of us had such strong feelings about the quality we didn't want to see it dragged out.'

Men Behaving Badly had lasted seven seasons and 42 episodes and it had changed the face of British situation comedy in the 1990s. But it finished at the right time – and with viewers wanting more. During its phenomenally successful run Martin's life had changed dramatically. He had gone into the series as a little known actor, but he came out of it as one of TV's brightest, most popular and most recognisable stars. He had also gone into the series married to Lucy Aston and emerged from it married to Philippa Braithwaite.

Looking back he was able to say: 'I do feel differently about marriage second time around. I don't even recognise myself from the man I was a few years ago.'

The series might have ended, but the public's appetite for *Men Behaving Badly* remained undiminished. Repeats subsequently pulled in big audiences, and demand for the DVDs remains healthy to this day. Clips on YouTube have registered hundreds of thousands of hits and the even the bloopers and outtakes continue to prove popular with users.

Such a loyal following leads to continuing speculation that *Men Behaving Badly* could return at some point, but when quizzed on the subject Martin has always ruled it out. He felt that two men in their forties behaving badly would appear 'seedy'. But he is realistic enough to say, 'If Simon Nye were to write something, then never say never.'

Nye had thought about an irrevocable demise for the four main characters by having them all burned to death in a barn. But as the show's most devoted fans keep telling themselves even now, theoretically they could all return one day.

A follow-up was genuinely mooted a few years ago when

the BBC were said to have offered Martin, Neil, Leslie and Caroline a reported £250,000 each to film three special programmes reuniting the characters. But Caroline Quentin was not in favour. Her career had moved on apace and a return to the role of Dorothy would probably have been seen as a backward step for her.

The suggestion then arose of a *Men Behaving Badly* spin-off featuring Martin and Neil but without the girls. Martin felt that would be missing the point completely. 'It's best,' he said, 'if we are left thinking that it would be nice if we all got back together, but then not actually do it.'

The series was re-made for American television but with an American cast, and eventually this led to the screening of the original on BBC America as *British Men Behaving Badly*. The series proved to have such international appeal that it was eventually seen in more than 50 countries, ranging from Brazil to Bulgaria, from Iceland to India, from Thailand to Trinidad.

One of the show's lasting legacies has been the continuing friendship between the four principal cast members. 'There was a love between us all in those days,' Neil recalls, 'and there still is. The feelings we had for each other were really strong. We were well bonded, we found each other and enjoyed each other's company to that extent.'

Leslie Ash commented: 'We felt as if we'd been to school together then left school and then all grown up. It was the most brilliant job. To have such a good time and to look forward going into work and just having a laugh, there's nothing better.' Leslie's ongoing screen storyline romance with Neil led to the pair teaming up for a series of lucrative advertisements for the DIY chain Homebase.

Martin has maintained a very special friendship with Caroline Quentin – they both have young daughters called Emily, and they have been on family holidays together in the Maldives. On a professional level, they also gelled splendidly once more in 1994 in a well received TV adaptation of *An Evening With Gary Lineker*, a play by Arthur Smith and Chris England which had first stormed the Edinburgh Fringe in 1991 before transferring successfully to London's West End.

Caroline starred as Monica, a woman on holiday in Spain during the 1990 World Cup with her husband Bill, a publisher, and his ghastly friend Ian. Long-suffering Monica comes a clear second best to her husband's love of football, especially when the men want to watch the semi-final between England and West Germany on television. They are joined for the viewing of the game by Bill's debonair best-selling author and Stoke City fanatic Dan, played by Martin.

The increasingly tense relationships between them all are played out in front of the television set. Monica gains revenge on her husband by having an affair with Dan, who is revealed to be a chauvinist writer whose passion for his best friend's wife is only eclipsed by his passion for football.

The comedy film was made in Ibiza and proved to be a most enjoyable shoot for Martin, Caroline and the rest of the cast, which included Clive Owen as Caroline's husband Bill and Paul Merton, then Caroline's real life husband, as the awful Ian.

The relationship between Martin and Neil also remains the strongest of bonds. The two actors have holidayed together with their respective other halves, and they enjoyed themselves hugely when they were commissioned to travel to Australia for a documentary series produced by Martin's new girlfriend Philippa Braithwaite, in which they explored the essence of Australian manhood in *Men Down Under*.

The mini-series had the pair following the route of the Olympic flame prior to Australia's hosting of the Olympic Games, and the aim was to find out if there was any truth in the British perception that the typical Aussie man was not much more than a macho, Fosters-drinking, crocodile-wrestler in a hat with dangling corks who ate kangaroo for lunch.

The duo started off at Ayers Rock before travelling on to Alice Springs to meet the golf-mad mayor and the men of Thursday Island. Subsequent episodes took them on a visit to Katherine, an oasis in the middle of nowhere, and a meeting with the testosterone-fuelled rodeo riders of the Norstock Bullriding challenge. Gary and Tony would have appreciated the fact that these men regarded the number of women they had in tow to be as important as their ability to stay on the back of wildly bucking broncos.

Martin and Neil completed their adventure by visiting Surfer's Paradise on the Gold Coast, taking in an Aussie Rules football game in Melbourne, visiting a koala park sanctuary in Sydney, and joining 35 marching drag queens in Sydney's gay and lesbian Mardi Gras. Martin and Neil were given a warm welcome wherever they went, an indication of how popular *Men Behaving Badly* had proved when screened in Australia. They were constantly asked for autographs and Martin was particularly amused – at Neil's expense – when one fan asked Martin for his autograph but totally failed to recognise Neil standing by.

If *Men Down Under* came across as a jolly jaunt, the highly imaginative comedy drama *Hunting Venus* (1999) was very different. It proved to be Martin's most interesting collaboration with his great friend, not least because it afforded Neil the chance to get right away from his *Men Behaving Badly* image by playing a transsexual.

The film was produced by Philippa Braithwaite and directed by Martin, who was the star of the piece. In pre-production there was much merriment between the couple as they mulled over exactly how big they should make Neil's fake boobs. 'They were very good,' Martin was eventually able to say with a hearty laugh of approval. 'They even swung when he walked!'

The seeds of the *Hunting Venus* project were sown when Martin and Neil agreed to get all dolled up to play the Ugly Sisters in a pantomime sketch for the BBC's fund-raising effort for Children In Need. Nick Vivian, husband of actress Jane Horrocks, who wrote the sketch, was so pleased with the outcome that he was of a mind to take it further and duly came up with a script which took an amusing and wry look at the New Romantic music scene of the 1980s.

This was a period when UK pop bands like Spandau Ballet,

Culture Club, Duran Duran, Adam and the Ants, and Steve Strange of Visage cultivated a dreamy, narcissistic look of extravagantly teased hair, eyeliner and other make-up, coupled with flamboyant foppish frills and colourful clothes made from luscious fabrics.

The central character of Vivian's screenplay for *Hunting Venus* featured Martin as Simon Delancey, the former guitarist of fictional one-hit-wonder 1980s band The Venus Hunters. Simon is introduced as a small-time con-man now fleecing old ladies in their homes. After relieving one gullible pensioner of her jewellery and other valuables, he checks into a seaside boarding house B & B to avoid the police, only for the landlady Cassandra to recognise him instantly as the pop star she once idolised and obsessively continues to do so.

Having booked him in, she hastily phones her friend Jacqui to tell her about her latest guest. It transpires that Cassandra and Jacqui, later revealed as lesbian lovers, ran the band's fan club which had ultimately resulted in their financial ruin. Together the two diehard fans contrive to kidnap Simon and blackmail him into tracking down the other four members of the band to reform the group, 16 years after they had split, for a reunion gig to be televised live. The problem is that some of the band haven't seen each other since they disbanded, and they loathe each other.

Martin stepped enthusiastically into the role of Simon and also set about recruiting some of the biggest names from the world of 1980s pop to make cameo appearances and give the film a measure of authenticity. He planned to have the likes of Simon Le Bon from Duran Duran, Tony Hadley of Spandau Ballet and Gary Numan appear as themselves in a sequence involving the re-formed Venus Hunters' rousing musical finale.

Martin sent scripts to each of the pop stars with covering letters asking them to get in touch if they were interested in adding their considerable presence to the movie. In truth he didn't hold out a lot of hope, but to his surprise and delight it took just four days for Gary Numan to sign up. Martin had long been a genuine fan of Numan's music, right from the days when he had first emerged as one of the pioneers of electronic pop with big hits like *Are Friends Electric?* and *Cars*.

Tony Hadley, Spandau Ballet's lead singer, by then forging a career as a solo singer, also declared he was happy to appear in *Hunting Venus*. He gave his agreement without even bothering to read the script.

Jools Holland, keyboard star with the band Squeeze as well as a noted television presenter, and Human League's lead singer Phil Oakey also readily signed up. Holland also provided original music for the show. Once Martin had spent some considerable time tracking down Simon Le Bon, the Duran Duran frontman was sweet-talked over a convivial dinner into coming on board.

Martin was thrilled by the willingness of such noted pop stars to take part in his movie, especially as the film would afford plenty of scope for sartorial satire in the band's reunion. Martin was to be dressed up in satin pantaloons, with a fetching earring dangling down the right side of his face and on the other his two-tone hair combed forward over one eye in the distinctive style of Phil Oakey.

Under Martin's purposeful direction, Neil emerged as the film's scene-stealer as the band's one-time heartthrob Charlie – by now a post-operative transsexual club singer called Charlotte.

Martin was confident his great pal would rise to the cross-dressing challenge and gave him full licence to make the most of the role. Neil submitted himself to fully five hours in make-up on the days when he was filmed in a strapless dress. He also uncomplainingly accepted that his hair extensions were non-removable at the end of each day: they had to remain a fixture for the duration of filming. 'He also had to have his nails done and his whole body shaved, so it was quite a commitment on his part,' said Martin.

The line-up of the band was completed by Mark Williams as the keyboard player who had gone on to become a high-flying businessman, Danny Webb as the bassist, now a plumber, and Ben Miller as the disturbed drummer, now confined to a mental institution.

Miller was impressed by Martin's direction. 'I found him really inventive,' he said. 'He did one tracking shot around Neil Morrissey, which is incredibly difficult because, as the camera moves, so does the entire crew. Seeing 50 blokes with pot bellies doing this ballet round the room was a fantastic moment.'

The crowning moment for Martin came after filming was completed. Gary Numan invited the actor to join him up on stage to play bass at his concert at Shepherd's Bush Empire. The 2,000-strong crowd gave Martin a rousing welcome which went some way to calming his nerves as Gary and the other members of his band swung into Gary's 1979 chart-topper *Cars*. Martin acquitted himself capably enough and was able to walk off stage with applause ringing in his ears, his head held high – and an ambition achieved.

Hunting Venus was enough of a success for big-money offers to be waved in front of Martin and the other members of The Venus Hunters to make an album. But Martin was shrewd enough to realise it would simply be falling into the trap of believing in the characters they were all playing.

CHAPTER 7

STAGGERED – AND SMITTEN

'We had to be secretive about our romance for fear of being considered unprofessional'
MARTIN ON FALLING FOR PRODUCER PHILIPPA BRAITHWAITE
WHILE MAKING THE FILM STAGGERED

It's a moment Martin Clunes can never, ever forget. There he was, standing stark naked on a remote Scottish island, freezing cold, and being watched closely by a camera crew and two of the most important women in his life.

On location for the film *Staggered*, Martin's character, hapless toy demonstrator Neil Price, was waking to the ultimate stag night prank. A jealous rival, played by Michael Praed, had drugged him, stripped him of all his clothes and had him flown by helicopter to the shivering shores of Barra in the Outer Hebrides.

It was a hard scene for any actor to undertake, but Martin's plight was made all the worse by the fact that in real life he was falling in love with the film's producer, Philippa Braithwaite, and he was acting with the inspirational Virginia McKenna, a lady he had been totally in awe of for most of his adult life.

Not only that, he was directing the movie himself after some last-minute personnel alterations which meant that there was absolutely no way he could get out of taking off his clothes, whatever the temperature or whoever was watching.

'I suppose it was the ultimate test,' said Martin soon after filming. 'Being left without a stitch was such a crucial part of the story that I just couldn't not do it. I needed the crew to respect and follow me for the full six weeks of the shoot so I had to put up with the cold, which turned my lips blue, and the monumental embarrassment.

'It was the first week of shooting and I had a lot of things to prove, so I couldn't really baulk there. I knew I'd have to do it sooner or later, get my kit off and sit in the Atlantic. I did manage to keep certain parts covered. I just stripped off, bared my bum and just about everything else and got on with it.'

Martin and Philippa had been just good friends before *Staggered* went into production. They had shared a healthy respect for each other as actor and producer respectively. But that all changed as the romance blossomed as the movie was made.

That fine actor John Forgeham, who played the deeply aggressive policeman hot on Neil Price's tail (his ruthless rival had also thoughtfully framed him for the theft of a thousand Sonic the Hedgehogs!) said: 'We had no idea that they were on the way to becoming an item. There are all sorts of liaisons during film-making and there's an old saying between actors and crew that when it comes to relationships, "Nothing counts on location." But obviously it counted for them.'

Martin himself was surprised by the suddenly increasing depth of his feelings for his pretty producer. 'At the time our romance was secret and it was all very intense so I barely noticed the beauty of the island of Barra itself,' he said. 'Philippa and I had some wonderfully romantic moments. We had to be secretive about our romance for fear of being considered unprofessional and distracting to those with whom we were working as she was the producer of the movie and I was the director as well as the leading man.'

The couple's first date had been arranged during pre-production of *Staggered*. Martin had been quite taken by his attractive producer and recalled: 'Her parents had some tickets for *Jurassic Park* and she asked me if I would like to come too. I said excitedly, "What, on a date?" and realised I'd said the wrong thing. But we went to see *Jurassic Park* at Leicester Square, just as we were about to make our own modest little English film.'

Both Martin and Philippa have said it was not quite love at first sight. 'We were both in a different place, as it were, when we first caught sight of each other,' he said. 'But she's a very attractive woman, so I spotted that.'

Philippa later said in an interview: 'We were both working and I was very focused on the film. Having any sort of relationship just didn't occur to me. But, because we worked together on the film for such a long time, it happened gradually. It all turned out well.'

Apart from the shocking early scene where Neil wakes up stark naked, there was also what Martin called gravely 'the Virginia McKenna factor'. The glacially beautiful actress and passionate spokeswoman for the animal world played a strange old Scottish woman who lived alone on the island for what she described as 'religious reasons'. She had failed to be accepted as a nun and shut herself away in isolation. She was kind, but shrewd enough to help Neil get a step nearer civilisation after separating him from his only remaining possession – his wristwatch.

Martin admitted later that he was quite overwhelmed by the prospect of acting with Ms McKenna. '*Born Free* was the first film I saw as a child,' he said. 'It made a huge impression on me. Virginia McKenna was a great heroine of mine, a wonderful actress and a fine wildlife campaigner and here I was working with her on *Staggered*. Not only that, I had to run naked towards her across the beach… I understand she is over the trauma now, but only just.'

The film was nicknamed *One Wedding and an Autopsy* as Neil's journey back to London involved a hilarious adventure with a romantic pathologist, played by Anna Chancellor. But there was little chance the movie could really rival the spectacularly successful *Four Weddings and a Funeral* and its comparatively enormous budget.

But there were real ambitions for *Staggered*. Martin said: 'There was a conscious effort to make a British film that did not involve the class structure but was just an ordinary film for ordinary people, just an entertainment. I wanted to make a film that was classless, contemporary and accessible. Popular is almost a dirty word in England. Sometimes I think film-makers want to retain some sort of exclusivity. *Staggered* is not like that. It's light, funny and will appeal to everybody.'

Certainly much of the action was hilarious, particularly when Neil got involved with a weird Welsh sexual swinger played by Griff Rhys Jones.

After it was all put together Jones went round to Martin's flat to watch a rough cut of the movie with Philippa. Martin remembers: 'One of the red-tops camped outside the flat and took a picture of her. The headline was: "Blonde Bombshell in TV Lout's London Love Nest". I thought, "OK, that's my girlfriend and my flat."' And they've been together ever since.

Life as an independent film maker is never easy and Philippa valued Martin's support on *Staggered* a great deal. She said: 'He has been with me all the way and without his backing I'm not sure I would have carried on. Although his acting career was going really well, he wanted to see me succeed, too.'

Martin was at the very peak of his *Men Behaving Badly* fame when he decided to ask Philippa to marry him. After the collapse of his marriage to Lucy Aston, he had sworn that he would never marry again. But he had made that vow when he was still emotionally battered and battle-scarred and now he was a very different man. His divorce from Lucy after three years of marriage had come through in 1996, and he made up his mind to pop the question to Philippa while he was on a working holiday in Hawaii filming a spot for the BBC's *Holiday* programme.

Martin was staying on the island of Maui, regarded by many as the loveliest of the Hawaiian islands, and not just because of its gorgeous palm-fringed beaches of white powdery sand and the sight of humpback whales frolicking far off shore. As Martin soon learned, Maui is also famed for one of the most breathtaking drives on Earth through a rainforest to Hana. The road takes in more than 600 curves, 54 one-lane bridges, spectacular cliffs, beautiful waterfalls, bamboo jungles, pineapple fields, tropical streams and pools, glorious fragrant flowers and lush vegetation.

How much more enjoyable would these glorious surroundings be, he thought, if Philippa was there to share them with him? He had known it for a while, but now it confirmed that he wanted spend the rest of his life with Philippa. And as a backdrop for a man to propose marriage to the girl he loved, Martin knew he could hardly choose better than Maui. Soon he was to have the opportunity to do so.

Since Martin and Philippa had fallen in love, the couple had spent very little time apart. Philippa had moved into Martin's London flat in Queenhithe and his trip to Hawaii represented the longest separation they had endured in their relationship – all of ten days. Martin was missing Philippa desperately and looking forward to her arrival to join him in Maui at the end of his filming stint, just as they had arranged.

Philippa finally arrived and fell into Martin's arms

completely exhausted after a flight which had amounted to 16 hours. She was whisked straight to the hotel where Martin was staying and as soon as the porter had delivered her luggage to their room and shut the door behind him, Martin excitedly asked Philippa to marry him. His proposal took Philippa's breath away. She said yes immediately, although Martin later joked that she was so jet-lagged from the long flight that she could hardly refuse.

At that point Martin had no engagement ring to present to Philippa, but as a symbol of their troth they bought a stone locally and the real thing at Tiffany's on Rodeo Drive in Los Angeles a few weeks later.

It was the perfect start to a romantic holiday in the most romantic of settings, and they immediately started making plans for their wedding. As Martin had been married before, they decided they would officially tie the knot in a civil ceremony and then have their marriage blessed in a church ceremony the following day. It would be as traditional a wedding as possible, given it was second time round for Martin.

Martin and Philippa formally became man and wife on 8 August 1997, at Finsbury Town Hall register office with Neil Morrissey as Martin's best man. Martin tried hard to keep the nuptials a secret but, as news of the wedding reached just one tabloid newspaper, he was relieved that the ceremony was far from the media circus he had feared. He even managed to avoid being photographed by hiding his face behind a large oblong wedding gift wrapped in gold paper.

It was a simple, low-key midday ceremony attended by just 20 guests, including actress Liz Carling. There was no official photographer on hand to record the union. The formalities over, the newlyweds then repaired to a top London restaurant with around 20 guests for a celebratory lunch before going their separate ways to spend the night apart – Martin escorted by Neil to the Savoy hotel while Philippa went back to their flat in the City.

Next morning Neil escorted Martin to historic St. Bride's church in Fleet Street. Philippa was driven there by car for a moving service in which their marriage was blessed in front of family and friends. At the lavish reception which followed, Leslie Ash, Caroline Quentin and Griff Rhys Jones were among the guests who toasted the couple before they left for their honeymoon. Not long afterwards, the newlywed would be resuming his role as Gary Strang, one of Britain's best-loved fictional bachelors.

As well as becoming man and wife, Martin and Philippa teamed up to form their own production company, Buffalo Pictures. The company apparently gained its name from the fact that Martin's date of birth was in the year of the Buffalo. The couple set up their company offices in Soho, just a short journey from the flat in Queenhithe that was now their marital home. It seemed a logical step for an in-demand actor-director and a successful producer to join forces to work on their own projects. As was later to become evident with a string of hits under the Buffalo banner, it was a smart move.

It was Martin's good fortune to be enjoying his

phenomenal success in *Men Behaving Badly* just at a time when he was given the opportunity to buy the flat in Queenhithe. He had never bought bricks and mortar before, but the regular sizeable income he was now receiving from the show meant that when the flat came up for sale, he was able to jump at the chance to buy it for £150,000.

Martin had made the flat a cosy habitat for himself and Philippa, but now he had secured ownership he was able to use his DIY and carpentry skills to turn it into a delightful home. This included putting in a smart new bathroom and a window seat shaped like a horseshoe around a circular table, where they could sit and watch the comings and goings on the river.

The flat proved to be not just a smart and comfortable residence but also a first home for the Cocker Spaniel, Mary, they soon acquired. It was also briefly a first home for their daughter Emily, when she was born in 1999. But with a dog and a small baby, Martin and Philippa had outgrown the flat and they decided to sell up and look for a house with a garden.

During the seven years Martin had lived in Queenhithe, the area had smartened up considerably and he was able to sell his flat for £450,000. This represented a very handsome profit and mirrored the remarkable change in his fortunes, both personally and professionally, from when he had first moved in.

Back in 1993 Martin had arrived at 419 Queen's Quay as a tenant seeking his own space after a broken marriage and as an insecure actor fretting over a TV series that had been cancelled. Now he was a very happily married man with a new wife he loved passionately, a new baby he doted on, a new pet he adored – and he was one of television's biggest stars. He left the flat with many memories to cherish.

Martin's new home was a Victorian terrace house in Putney, in south west London, not far from the bachelor flat he had shared with pals after leaving drama school and only a few miles from Wimbledon Common where he had grown up. It was a reminder of just how far he had come in life.

CHAPTER 8

NEVILLE'S ISLAND

'It was very cold and you feel so exposed'
MARTIN ON SPENDING FOUR DAYS BEING FILMED
UP A TREE IN JUST HIS UNDERPANTS

Originally commissioned by Alan Ayckbourn for his Scarborough theatre, Tim Firth's dark comedy *Neville's Island* – about four middle-aged businessmen on an ill-fated team-building weekend in the Lake District – was a huge success in the theatre.

The ruthless competition between the four outward-bounders was a hit up and down the country, so by the time the decision was taken to film a television version, expectations were high. Viewers were promised a story that was a cross between *Lord of the Flies* and *Deliverance*. So no pressure then for ITV, who were determined the quirky play could be a small-screen success. 'I'm a big fan of Tim Firth,' said ITV's comedy controller Paul Spencer. 'You could see straight away it would make a great film.'

As Neville himself says as the curious quartet head off from civilisation: 'They make films about this, don't they? People go on islands, become shipwrecked and what happens is they gradually go back to nature and shed 20th-century values and tell each other dark secrets that release hidden qualities.'

The theatre version had to be slimmed down by about half to fit into a 90-minute slot on ITV. Timothy Spall and Jeff Rawle were already in the West End cast, but when David Bamber, Martin Clunes and Sylvia Syms came on board the prospects of real ratings success grew.

ITV were delighted to have secured the services of Martin, who was by then seen as a BBC star. In fact, the BBC had rejected the chance to televise *Neville's Island*. An anonymous ITV executive said: 'We're as pleased as punch to have signed him up for this.'

Martin was to play the role of simple, religious Roy, the worker who has suffered a nervous breakdown and found God. After a tongue-lashing from cruel, sarcastic Gordon, played by Timothy Spall, he climbs a tree and sits on a branch in his underpants, clutching a machete and singing 'Morning has Broken' over and over again.

When Neville (Jeff Rawle) tries to talk him down he finds himself listening to a shocking confession. Roy reveals he has murdered his mother. When he explains, it is clear he had in fact only turned off her life-support machine, on medical advice. But the impact on poor confused Roy was just as severe as if he had been a fully blown killer. He seems to have decided to commit suicide by hanging himself from the tree. Instead he catches a huge falcon, kills it, wrenches its innards out then serves it to his starving pals with his bare hands.

It was certainly very different from most roles he had played, said Martin, with a degree of understatement. 'He is unstable but very God-fearing. I am not religious at all, but I do have beliefs, so it was not hard to get inside the head of someone who believes in things so passionately. With a script this strong an actor just can't really go wrong.'

For the role, Martin was called upon to assume a Northern accent, which he pitched somewhere between Manchester and Leeds and just about got away with it. Filming took place on beautiful Derwentwater in the Lake District in October and November 1997. It looked beautiful but the weather was freezing. Martin, who again had to strip almost naked in one scene, certainly found that the cold weather was a challenge. He remarked afterwards that it took four days to film the scene where Roy was up the tree in his underpants. 'It was very cold and you feel so exposed,' he said. He was delighted to be playing the character with fewest funny lines for once.

The actors found that the 10-week shoot was like the story of the film, except that they had a film crew on hand and got to go back to their warm and comfortable hotel every night. But the whole cast and crew were deeply impressed by the stunning natural backdrop. 'The Lake District was an incredibly beautiful location to make a film,' said Martin. 'I'll never forget the end of one day's shooting. It was round about dusk and we were heading back up the lake on this little putt-putt boat. The water was completely still. It was one of those golden autumnal evenings and ahead of us was a small island surrounded by cormorants. It was one of those moments when there's nowhere else you would rather be.'

Martin was called upon to take his clothes off in a very different way, in a BBC2 drama about wife-swapping called *Touch and Go* alongside Zara Turner, Ewan Stewart and Teresa Banham. Martin played Nick Wood who, with his wife Angela (Zara Turner), experiments with exchanging sexual partners to try to rescue their ailing marriage.

There was much more to this 50-minute film than cheap thrills to cash in on the popularity of Martin's comedy character. The script rang with such truth it frightened him into agreeing to play the part. He explained: 'Most of the stuff I am shown is sub-standard *Men Behaving Badly*, but this is really well written and it scared me so much I thought I would do it. What is interesting about *Touch and Go* is the way it explores the collapse of a relationship. Wife-swapping is the backdrop to this. It offers itself as a solution and for a split second it looks as if it might work.'

After finishing filming Martin said that it had been the 'toughest job I've ever done, because of the place I had to put my head.' He had to inhabit the decline of a relationship and said that there were moments of such despair in the script that it reduced him to real tears. He also admitted later that his wife Philippa was upset by the more revealing scenes in the film. 'She doesn't like it,' said Martin. 'But she knows it is my job. She is very good about it, but quite understandably doesn't like the thought of saying, "What did you do at work today, dear?"'

CHAPTER 9

AN ELEPHANT
CALLED NINA

'I was quite nervous — I'd never met an elephant before.
Well, you don't if you grow up in Wimbledon, do you?'
MARTIN ON HIS INTRODUCTION TO NINA
THE ELEPHANT IN AFRICA

Martin was just five years old when he was taken to the cinema to see the film *Born Free*, the heart-warming story of a British couple in Africa who, at the maturity of their pet lioness, educate the beast to survive in the bush.

The 1966 film was an adaptation of Joy Adamson's true story of how she and her husband George, played by Virginia McKenna and Bill Travers, involuntarily domesticated several pet lions. They kept one, Elsa, until she was fully grown and then, to save her from government-ordered captivity, trained her to survive as a wild animal.

The film was a massive box office hit and, like many a youngster who went to see it, Martin watched spellbound as the tale unfolded on the screen. It made such an impression that he went on to read the books *Born Free*, *Living Free* and *Forever Free* which chronicled Elsa's story.

The second film Martin can remember seeing is *Ring of*

Bright Water starring the same two actors in an engaging tale about an otter, based on Gavin Maxwell's autobiographical bestseller. Travers played a London civil servant anxious to get out of the rat race, who acquires Mij, a young otter, as a pet but soon finds that keeping the charming but mischievous mammal in a London apartment is fraught with problems. So he leaves London for a lonely coastal village in the Highlands of Scotland, where he settles down in a crofter's cottage in an environment where Mij can grow and lead a natural life.

Born Free and *Ring of Bright Water* left an indelible mark upon young Martin, but he can never have dreamed that one day he would not only act alongside Virginia but direct her in a movie which would be produced by his wife and filmed in otter country in the wilds of Scotland.

As we have seen, *Staggered* was the movie that introduced Martin to Virginia – it was the first time she had been back in the Highlands since *Ring of Bright Water* – and the two subsequently became good friends. 'It was very special meeting her,' said Martin, citing an instant rapport. 'She's an inspiring lady, and that was when I became aware of the Born Free Foundation which Virginia founded.'

Born Free is an international charity working throughout the world to stop wild animal suffering and to protect threatened species in the wild. Having been a loyal supporter for some 15 years, Martin is now a patron.

At first his association with Born Free involved some PR and adding his name to various awareness and fund-raising campaigns. But in 1998 he was approached by Born Free about presenting and featuring in a documentary about the rescue of an orphaned baby elephant and its subsequent rehabilitation back into the wild.

For 26 of her 27 years, Nina the elephant had lived in a private zoo in Kenya. But when it was announced that the zoo was to close, Nina's owner approached Born Free for their help in taking on an untried task – returning to the wild a fully grown tame elephant which had been captive for so many years.

This was something that had never been attempted before, and several animal experts doubted whether it would be possible after Nina had spent such a long time in captivity, cared for and attended by humans. But with Nina clearly frustrated by captivity and longing for companions of her own kind, Born Free decided it was well worth a try.

As an animal lover Martin had no second thoughts when asked to become involved in the project. This was his chance to make a real difference and to do something thoroughly worthwhile for Born Free in a documentary, which would be filmed for the BBC's popular *Born to be Wild* TV series.

Even before Martin flew out to Africa to meet Nina, Born Free put a great deal of effort into raising funds for the project and assembling a team of experts. Moving a four-and-a-half ton elephant 180 miles through Kenya across the border to the Mkomazi Game Reserve in northern Tanzania presented a host of logistical problems and required meticulous planning. Everyone agreed that Nina's move would only go ahead if her welfare was the top priority.

For Martin it was virtually love at first sight when he was introduced to Nina at the Mount Meru Game Sanctuary prior to her relocation. Like a self-conscious teenager unsure of himself on a first date, he stepped gingerly forward with a gift – some bananas, which were received with relish by Nina before she checked him out with her snout. 'I was quite nervous,' Martin admitted. 'I'd never met an elephant before. Well, you don't if you grow up in Wimbledon, do you?'

The formalities over, Nina and Martin in time went on to develop a mutual affection over his three visits made to Africa specifically to see her.

The attempt to move the elephant began at 6.30 one March morning with Martin and Nina under the eye of a BBC film crew as the team tried to coax Nina into a vast crate. It proved a fruitless exercise – she was having none of it. Even Martin's bait of bananas and a few tongue-clicking noises by way of encouragement failed to lure Nina into the transporter.

'Having started to win Nina's affections with cupboard love, it seemed churlish not to help her in her hour of need,' Martin later reported. 'I made the clicking noises whenever I fed her. I thought I could encourage some sort of Pavlovian response.'

Ten hours of pushing, shoving, cajoling and bribery passed but all to no avail. Nina stubbornly refused to budge. With time now running out, the decision was made to tranquilise her and, once the drugs had taken effect and she'd subsided on to her side, Nina was lifted on to a low-loader and then into Born Free's massive relocation truck, aptly named Hannibal, which had been donated to the Kenya Wildlife Service.

During Nina's journey along 180 miles of road, she lay on her side and Martin took up a position between her front legs and her jaw so that he could perform the vital task of holding her trunk straight to allow her to breathe freely.

The road trip proved arduous and hazardous, frequently hampered by traffic and the negotiation of low cable lines. But it finally ended with Nina's safe arrival at the Mkomazi Game Reserve, run by Tony Fitzjohn who has dedicated his life to saving endangered species in East Africa.

A noted conservationist, Tony had worked with George Adamson for 18 years until the latter was murdered. During their remarkable working partnership they successfully reintroduced into the wild more than 30 lions and 10 leopards. Together they also pioneered the development and management of the Kora National Park in Kenya, and Tony owes George his life. 'He saved Tony's life when he was attacked by a wild lion,' Martin explains. 'The wound was so deep he could put a hand right through his collar bone, and he still has the scars.'

It was at once clear that Nina was in good hands. During the 1980s the huge elephant herds had been decimated through poaching and reduced to just 11 individuals. But aided by an ivory ban and increased security within Mkomazi under Tony Fitzjohn's conservation programme, the elephant count is now around 1,000 in the wet season.

Martin and the team were relieved that the first aim of

Project Nina had been achieved. She had survived the journey remarkably well all things considered, but the team were all aware that there was much more to be done before they could achieve their ultimate objective.

While Nina became acclimatised to her new surroundings, she could now hear, for the first time since she was orphaned at six months old, the sounds of the wild, including other elephants.

The next task was to wean Nina off the diet of bananas and sugar cane, to which she had long been accustomed, and to teach her to feed on the vegetation she would eventually find out in the wilderness. Only then could the team be confident she could survive in the 150-square-mile game reserve at the foot of Mount Kilimanjaro where animals roam protected from poachers.

While Nina was prepared for her new world, Martin and the rest of the team left her at the reserve, returning in April to witness her release into the wild. But they were to be disappointed.

Perhaps it was not altogether unexpected, but Nina stayed close to the camp to begin with, showing little inclination to step out of her comfort zone. Initially she was so used to being around humans that she did not appear interested in wandering very far away, despite being given every encouragement to do so.

But all that changed seven and a half weeks later, when two male bull elephants wandered into the camp, probably drawn to its waterhole. When they left later that day, Nina tagged along with them, much to the relief and joy of Martin and the Born Free team. There was great jubilation that she had taken her first steps to freedom.

Three months later, in September, Martin flew to Africa for a third time to bid a final farewell to his friend. Joining up with the team again, they spent days tracking Nina in the bush. Just watching elephants in their natural habitat reinforced Martin's love for them. He marvelled at their essentially gentle nature and the way they played together and stayed together as a family.

Finally Martin and the team caught sight of Nina. Now, however, she appeared cautious and tentative about approaching humans and vehicles. That was a good sign, an indication that her repatriation into her own world had been successful.

Then she spotted Martin and he was visibly moved when she raised her huge trunk in recognition and greeting and slowly sauntered up to him to accept his parting gift of one final banana. Nina lingered with Martin for a few moments before ambling off once more. 'It was like our audience with her was over,' he recalled. 'I'll never forget seeing her disappear into the bush for the last time. I was a bit in love with Nina, but it was time to say goodbye.'

For Martin and the team, it was mission accomplished, and proof that after 20 years in a zoo an elephant can still successfully go back to the wild. As Born Free points out, this could be a solution for other elephants.

But that wasn't quite the end of the story. According to

rangers who kept an eye on her, Nina adapted well to the wild, learning how to forage for food and only occasionally retracing her steps to the release camp for water and a banana. Born Free learned that her tusks grew, she became big and strong and successfully linked up with different groups of wild elephants.

Then, one day during the dry season, Nina wandered back into the camp to drink at the waterhole. But this time she was not alone – she had brought her young son with her. Tony Fitzjohn, a big rugby fan, quickly named him Jonny Wilkinson after the England star – Nina had given birth to her calf on the same day in November 2003 when England beat Australia in Sydney to win the Rugby World Cup.

Martin and Born Free were thrilled when news was relayed to them that Nina had become a mother. They could hardly have hoped for more.

When the film of Martin's mission was screened by the BBC in *Born to be Wild*, it was watched by an incredible 13 million viewers. Thanks to Martin's high profile in *Men Behaving Badly* and the genuine enthusiasm he displayed for the project while promoting the film prior to transmission, Nina's story caught the public imagination. It also helped put the Mkomazi Game Reserve on the map to the extent that it was later reclassified as a national park, giving its long-term protected status additional security.

Sadly, however, in October 2007, Nina died. Rangers had noticed one day that she was looking unwell and ill at ease and next day her body was found just about a kilometre from the area where she had been released.

It transpired she had actually died in labour. Born Free reported: 'The autopsy showed that the calf being round the wrong way was the cause of her death. This is a tragic but not an especially rare condition which has been known to cause fatality in otherwise healthy wild elephants.'

Martin was able to console himself that he had contributed to Nina enjoying 10 years of freedom in her natural habitat and that she had died trying to give birth to another calf rather than being shot by poachers. 'I still feel extremely privileged to have spent time with Nina,' he said, 'and I try to help Born Free whenever I can.

'Being directly involved in animals does the soul good. It reminds you that humans are just another species on this planet.'

Martin carried this message further when he went on to narrate another TV documentary which highlighted the plight of a thousand bears who were forced to live in confinement across Japan's bear parks in conditions so squalid that they couldn't stand up.

Following his enchanting encounter with Nina, Martin remains a prominent campaigner for conservation of elephants, particularly in the light of a report in 2008 that the ivory trade may lead to the extinction of Africa's elephants by 2020. The report stated that the number of elephants roaming free had dwindled to fewer than 470,000 whereas there were around one million in the

1980s. The shocking statistics prompted Martin to do his bit in bringing them to the notice of a wider public.

CHAPTER 10

FATHER AND DAUGHTER

'I can't ever recall feeling such emotions'
MARTIN ON WITNESSING THE BIRTH OF
HIS DAUGHTER EMILY

M artin and his wife Philippa might have put together hours of top-rated television and some memorable feature films, but by far their most important production arrived on schedule in October 1999, in the shape of their beautiful baby daughter Emily Kate.

Mother and father were overjoyed by Emily's arrival. Martin enthused soon afterwards: 'I never thought of myself as a family sort of person before, but in the morning I wake up and there she is. And I have to say I am loving every minute of it.'

Martin and Philippa were watching an edition of *Pet Rescue* on television when she went into labour. They moved swiftly to the Portland Clinic in London where little Emily arrived after some 15 hours' labour.

Martin was deeply moved. 'I can't ever recall feeling such emotions,' he said. 'No matter how many preconceptions you have, nothing really prepares you for the actual second when your baby is born. First you have all the distress of seeing your partner in so much discomfort. Then suddenly it's all over and that distress is replaced by sheer joy.'

Martin was so overwhelmed by the birth of his daughter that, far from rushing down to the pub as his *Men Behaving Badly* character might have done, he stayed at the hospital overnight. He simply couldn't bear the idea of leaving his brand new family. 'Most men probably want to race away and light up a cigar when they become a dad for the first time,' he said. 'But I couldn't just say "Bye then" and take off. I had to be there for both of them for as long as possible.'

Instantly Martin turned into the most devoted dad imaginable. He doted on his lovely little daughter from the moment she was born. 'I still do,' he laughs. 'I guess I always will. I had no idea she would make such a change to my life.'

Martin cheerfully set out to share as many duties as possible with his wife and was soon boasting about his nifty nappy-changing skills to anyone who would listen. 'I'm really into being a dad,' said Martin, as he went round with an unshiftable beam on his face for what seemed like months.

Baby Emily certainly had a profound impact on Martin's life. One of the biggest benefits she brought was his decision to finally give up smoking. Martin used to smoke up to 40 cigarettes a day. When pressed on the subject he admitted he could even remember once lighting up in the toilet on an aeroplane and getting a severe reprimand from the angry cabin staff. 'I was a real shocker when it came to the old weed,' he said.

'But Emily's arrival has changed all that. As soon as you become a father yourself, you suddenly realise that you want to be around to see your own child grow up. So that was my spur to give up smoking. Emily has completely changed me. I'm being a very good boy and I'm really quite proud of myself.'

Although Martin knew absolutely he had to quit the habit, he admitted it was the hardest thing he'd ever had to do. He had smoked heavily since he was a teenager, and he particularly liked to smoke when he was filming. It was something to do to fill time in between the scenes. He also had to have a cigarette the minute he got in a car or finished a meal. Smoking was a big part of his daily routine.

Not long before Emily was born he had tried to give up while on a long family holiday. He managed to last out for three months but started again on his first day back in front of the cameras. There was such a strong association between filming and smoking that he felt he could not manage to get through the day without those cigarettes. 'Again I simply found it was impossible to stop,' he said.

'Even the fact that my father was a pipe smoker who died from lung cancer when I was eight couldn't convince me to stop. It became really frustrating.'

Close to his wits' end, Martin visited the therapist Allen Carr at his London clinic. Carr was himself an ex-smoker who had once chain-smoked more than 100 cigarettes a day. Martin listened to him for four and a half hours until Carr had managed to talk him out of it. 'He encouraged me to smoke while he explained that cigarettes don't give genuine pleasure or provide a reliable crutch,' said Martin. 'Once that was understood he had removed my need or desire to smoke.'

As a sign of his resolve, Martin handed over his packet of cigarettes and made a firm commitment to stop for good. At the end, Martin said, 'there was a bit of hypnosis, when he reiterated the points we had discussed to reinforce them in my mind.' Martin has not smoked since, and later Philippa undertook the same treatment and gave up too. 'It's the best money we've ever spent as it will lengthen our lives,' said Martin. He knew he owed it as a father to be a part of Emily's life for as long as possible.

However, although he has not been tempted to smoke again, Martin revealed that for a time he did seem to have replaced tobacco with food. As with many reformed smokers who find their sense of smell returning and their taste buds more naturally responsive, food suddenly started causing problems of its own!

Martin has also become a passionate anti-smoking campaigner. 'I'm a typical reformed smoker in that now I'm completely anti,' he says. 'And I get especially angry if anyone smokes around Emily. My family is so important to me.'

CHAPTER 11

MAN BEHAVING DIFFERENTLY

'Sex scenes are always the least sexy scenes you can do'
MARTIN CLUNES

After the huge and sustained success of *Men Behaving Badly*, Martin knew he wanted to do something completely different. Happily for him – or so it seemed at the time – the BBC had just the thing.

Over the years the BBC has made some inspired decisions when it comes to commissioning new dramas, but even the Corporation's most devoted fan could not claim that spending £10million filming *Gormenghast* was one of them. As the year 2000 finally dawned, the ambitious four-hour version of Mervyn Peake's Gothic fantasy trilogy was to be the compelling spearhead of the BBC's schedule for the new millennium.

Peake's novels certainly had a cult following but for many readers they represented a gloomy saga involving loneliness, suffering and evil. Martin was recruited as part of a stellar cast who included Jonathan Rhys Meyers, Stephen Fry,

Christopher Lee, Celia Imrie, Warren Mitchell and Zoe Wanamaker. Ian Richardson's character turned into an owl. Spike Milligan had a role that required him to be fired from a cannon. June Brown, better known as Dot Cotton from *EastEnders*, played the scary Nanny Slagg. Eric Sykes also appeared, with a large goat.

Producer Estelle Daniel was full of enthusiasm as *Gormenghast* went into production at Shepperton Studios. 'We've conceived it as a wonderful turn-of-the-century comedy,' she gushed. 'It's about the parting of an old age and the coming of a new. It's got action adventure. It's got romance. It's got comedy. There are three seductions, six murders and two tragic deaths!'

Unfortunately when it finally came to the screen what it did not have was enough viewers. It began with an armchair audience of more than four million but ended with fewer than half that number as people turned off from a drama that seemed confused and for many people impossible to follow. Jack Dee joked at an awards ceremony: 'I got drunk and watched *Gormenghast* and understood it.' Spike Milligan went public to say he couldn't bear to watch himself in the drama.

Martin was as baffled as many of the other performers when they watched the end result. His performance as Professor Flower escaped most of the catcalls and condemnation that other members of the cast received. That most perceptive of critics Nancy Banks-Smith said in the *Guardian*: 'Enter Eric Sykes with goat. It is a stage instruction worthy of Shakespeare. I was tempted back to *Gormenghast* this week by a star burst of comic talent. It was well hidden. I finally found Martin Clunes, the most mobile mouth in show business, lurking behind a large moustache.'

Most reviewers ridiculed the whole over-hyped project and even former BBC boss Paul Fox gave up after the first episode. 'It looks fantastic and has a wonderful cast, but it is totally inaccessible,' he admitted. 'Nobody else in the whole world apart from the BBC would have taken it on.' Martin decided to put *Gormenghast* down to experience. When asked shortly afterwards for his thoughts on the expensive production he smiled and said tactfully: 'Next question.'

Fortunately for Martin he was still very much in demand and an altogether more promising television project was on the way. Acclaimed crime writer and novelist Michael Dibdin, who died in 2007, is best remembered for his haunting, thoughtful stories of the Venice-born detective Aurelio Zen. But he also wrote a wonderfully inventive novel about sex, greed, and murder in Thatcher's Britain called *Dirty Tricks*.

The central character of Dibdin's hilarious and compelling page-turner is an amoral English tutor called Edward, who is charming, witty and successful with women while also being an accomplished liar, ruthlessly calculating and a born survivor. Edward is penniless but he's determined to use his smooth-talking appeal to the opposite sex to change that as quickly as possible.

Edward is seduced very early on in the piece by the insatiable Karen, the sex-crazed, gym-teacher wife of his boss's accountant Dennis. The earthy action takes place upstairs in the lavatory during an otherwise dull dinner party. The liaison sets in motion a tragic yet hilarious sequence of events that soon has Edward using all his guile and wide-eyed expression of innocence to avoid going to prison on a murder charge.

The screen potential of *Dirty Tricks* was obvious. A co-production was agreed between Little Bird and the ITV company Carlton, and the novel was skilfully adapted for the small screen by Nigel Williams. As Jonathan Powell, Carlton's director of drama, put it at the time: '*Dirty Tricks* is a very sexy story. It is a glorious mix of gripping thriller and savage comedy.'

The casting of Edward was crucial to the success of the project. It required an actor who could handle the raunchy, no-holds-barred sex scenes and the deviously callous disposal of the swiftly terminated Karen and subsequent framing of an innocent man for murder while still retaining the affection of the audience. Powell said at the time: 'Martin Clunes was perfect for the role. In fact, he was so perfect I don't think we could have gone with anyone else. It could have been written for him.'

Fortunately Martin agreed. He was understandably wary of playing roles that were simply another version of Gary from *Men Behaving Badly*. 'Gary was great,' said Martin. 'But it was very much of a case of been there, done that, with a lot of the scripts that I saw at the time. I wanted to move on and do something different. I soon realised that while Edward might have been described as behaving badly he was much, much worse than dear old Gary, and deeply different in many, many ways.'

The sexual side of the story was certainly strong stuff for a television audience. But Martin was not fazed by the sex scenes and said simply: 'It's adult entertainment, but adult entertainment of the highest quality. I get quite a few scripts sent to me featuring sub-*Men Behaving Badly* characters and old hat TV detectives, but this one stood out as being different, original and extremely entertaining. It's a thriller and a comedy and it's very dark. I love it.'

The number of nude scenes did cause Martin some concern. He had put on a little weight and wanted to look his best in the many scenes where he would be without his clothes. 'I hired a personal trainer,' he smiled. 'I wanted to try to make myself look less doughy. I wouldn't want anyone to think I was vain. I knew my bottom was going to be in view and I am very sorry to all viewers about that.

'It went well for a time and I was losing weight at a pretty pleasing rate. I got a bit hooked on exercising, which is something I never thought I would say. But then, just before we began filming, I lent over to kiss my daughter goodnight in her cot and something went in my back. The back went into spasm. I was crocked, and that was the end of my exercising, at least for a time. After looking forward to walking on set on the first day, looking slim and with a spring in my step, I sort of limped on feeling not exactly in prime condition.'

Not all of the Dibdin novel made it on to the screen, but Nigel Williams cleverly extracted a scintillating storyline that opened with Edward lying alone in bed, only to be totally traumatised by a knock on the door by two determined-looking detectives.

Williams used the sometimes awkward and stilted device of having his main character talking direct to camera to move along the story. In less expert hands, this jars and gets in the way of the action, but in Martin's hands this narration worked wonderfully well. 'I'm in a spot of bother with the law,' he explains in the opening scene with massive understatement. We soon learn that he is on the run, accused of murder and his face has been splashed all over the newspapers.

With the audience instantly hooked, the fascinating rewind to discover why our cheeky-faced hero was in such dire trouble begins. It all starts when, as 'a penniless teacher at a low-rent language school', he meets Karen and Dennis Parsons at an excruciating social evening at their large and comfortable suburban house. Edward is hardly looking for an illicit affair when Karen's foot snakes under the dinner table and begins to caress his groin. No one can accuse Karen of being subtle and she follows Edward upstairs to the toilet and pretty well forces herself on him.

Karen was played by Scottish actress Julie Graham and the screen chemistry between her and Martin was obvious to everyone from the start. 'Working with Martin was great fun,' said Julie. 'We had to do lots of sex scenes which are always the least sexy things you can do. But Martin was great at breaking the tension. He would fool around on set to get us all going.

'In one shot he even put my red bra on and started waving

at me through a window! As a result we were in hysterics most of the time we were working together. People think it must be embarrassing doing those scenes but there was never any embarrassment with Martin. And anyway it is all so technical. As you're in what is supposed to be a steamy clinch you have the director saying things like, "Can you move your eyeball to the right and your right ear to the left?"'

Edward responds quickly when Karen arrives in the toilet desperate to have sex, but he has no idea what he is getting himself into. 'Karen actually loves her husband but she is frantic to have a baby,' said Julie. Dennis is deeply dreary. He is an accountant who is forever boring people rigid with his lectures on interest-free mortgages and tax efficient investment and pretentious remarks about his knowledge of wine. 'He's always trying to climb up the social ladder with equally dull middleclass wannabes,' said Julie. Neil Dudgeon played the part with great style as he positively revelled in the role of the boorish, unattractive loudmouth.

Karen doesn't mind her husband's social inadequacies. Her biggest problem is that he is infertile while she desperately wants to have children. They no longer have sex although they still love each other in their own rather odd way. 'Karen has developed this fetish about having sex with other men – but only while Dennis is around,' Julie explained. 'In some confused kind of thinking, she doesn't feel she is really being unfaithful as long as her husband is there!'

The explicit sex scenes did not bother Martin either, except that he didn't exactly relish removing all his clothes for the cameras. 'You know when you turn up for the day's filming that there are sex scenes coming,' he said. 'So there comes that moment when you just have to grit your teeth and go for it. You just have to jump off the cliff. No one wants to show their bum really but it's just filming and part of the job. In this case it became very giggly quite often. I got on so well with Julie, and such a high regard for her as an actress, that it was great.

'I have done sex scenes with other actresses who would really rather not have taken part, and that makes it very difficult. So a lot of how it goes is down to the personalities of the people involved.' Martin's sense of humour saved any possible hint of awkwardness in spite of a few difficult moments. 'We once shot three sex scenes in one day and my arms ached at the end,' he said. 'You don't normally go on that long... well, I don't!'

'Fortunately,' said Martin, 'Julie was very relaxed about the whole thing. Because of the nature of the sex in the piece – it's stolen sex, quite heightened and even comic – it felt different from doing a full-on, steamy, love-filled, sex scene.' At least that was what he told his wife Philippa when he went off to work in the morning, he joked.

In fact Martin even made his own backless pants for one scene, which he stuck onto his bottom with toupee tape. 'The costume people go into overdrive to protect your modesty,' he said, 'but one day I really couldn't work out how to use what I had been presented with. It looked like a flesh-coloured kite made out of coathanger wire that really wouldn't bend the way I wanted to.' He cut the front out of a pair of pants and simply stuck it on himself and thought he had saved the costume department a job of work.

After Edward and Karen kick off their instant affair with passionate sex in the toilet, they come to an understanding that their torrid couplings will always be haunted by the presence of her hapless husband. It works well for a while with some X-certificate excitement for the viewers. But disaster strikes when Edward joins Dennis and Karen on a punting trip on the river. Just as Dennis is insisting he knows exactly what he is doing he falls in and drowns. This leaves the field clear for Edward to make his romantic move. He pushes himself forward and lets grieving Karen know that he is the man who can make her happy and become the father of her children – conveniently forgetting to inform her he had a vasectomy some years previously.

Edward moves into the lavish house but when he finds out Karen is being unfaithful to him all hell breaks loose. Karen is found dead after a night of bitter wrangling and Edward ruthlessly schemes to frame her other lover for the murder. He seems to have got away with it for a while, thanks to a brutal cop who beats a confession out of an innocent man. But the conviction is overturned, and Edward and his fortune are finally pursued to South America by the police. There might have been only a passing association with realism in the glossy two-parter but it was stylish and very well received.

Martin was absolutely delighted by the experience. 'I defy any actor to pass up an opportunity to play this character,' he laughed afterwards. 'He is the ultimate cad.'

'*Dirty Tricks* leapt out from all the other scripts that came my way,' he said. 'It was such an unusual screenplay to read. It is quite liberating to play someone so horrible and to have to lie so much. At the same time, all actors want to be loved – or at least I do – so it's harder to accept that I'll be disliked. But I suppose it makes a nice change to be playing someone who is more successful with women than Gary was. I always try not to judge the characters I play but Edward was totally pitiful!'

If anyone could play a completely immoral bastard while increasing his comedy profile it had to be Martin. He had no worries at all about playing yet another disreputable character. The enthusiasm to work and to work hard was too strong to even think about saying no. 'There comes a time where you think, "If I don't play him then someone else will." I might as well cash in while I am still getting sent them. Success is not supposed to last and that is something I think about, as a self-employed man with a family.'

Baby Emily had only just arrived when Martin turned up on television playing another sleazeball, in the unappetising shape of deeply immoral TV chat show host Ben Black in *Sex 'n' Death*. The original script called for Martin to appear completely naked in one scene but this time he refused. 'I haven't minded taking my clothes off in the past,' he said. 'But these days I am old and fat.'

Martin had to play a vile and anarchic television presenter who will do anything to improve his all-important ratings. Black, whose wife Bella (played by Caroline Goodall) was also his producer, introduced female religious mud-wrestling with Catholics, Protestants, Muslims and Jews fighting each other. As if that were not tasteless enough, he also tricks his audience into stripping off into the nude.

One grimly memorable scene featured Black clad only in a loincloth and a crown of thorns, and attached to a cross like Jesus. Martin was well aware that some viewers would find this shocking but he said: 'It is going to offend some people, but I am sure Christianity can stand it. Ben Black's show is not a million miles from TV today. It's just a step to the left of *Noel's House Party* – people setting other people up.'

But new father Martin admitted he did worry about the influence of television programmes on young and vulnerable children. 'I can imagine the kind of peer pressure there is already for children to have TV sets in their own rooms,' he said. 'The concern then is what kind of programmes they will be watching in the near future – a programme like *Sex 'n' Death*! Television was all pretty new when I was little. In fact we were one of the last people in our street to get one. Now children in ever the poorest families have their own set.'

The satirical black comedy certainly had Martin musing on the future of TV. With remarkable foresight he said: 'With diversification and endless channels, people will be able to choose exactly what kind of TV they watch. There could even be a Scalextric Channel for fans of toy car racing and it would get an audience! There will be more public access TV, more porn and shopping channels galore. There will also be good drama and quality programmes. People will have to choose what they want and not complain about the rest. All you have to do is switch off.'

But after the excesses of *Sex 'n' Death* it was time for a change of medium as well. Martin was anxious to find a way to stretch himself and to take his career, at least for a short period, in a new direction, so he agreed to star in the title role of Moliere's *Tartuffe* at the National Theatre.

It was a bold choice indeed. *Tartuffe* (or *The Imposter*) is the great French dramatist's most famous play, but it has always been difficult and controversial. Soon after it was written, back in the 17th century, the Archbishop of Paris was appalled by the anti-religious message he falsely believed it contained and threatened instant excommunication for anyone who watched, performed or even read the play.

The corrupt religious establishment could not stand the exposure of a con man and womaniser masquerading as a man of God. The savage satire on false piety and insufferable hypocrisy was banned for five years until Moliere used his influence with King Louis XIV to get permission for the play to be staged in public.

Martin knew that playing Tartuffe represented a massive challenge. He recognised that his high public profile would ensure that he would be right in the spotlight of searching examination of his performance, but he was determined to do it. As his agent said at the time: 'People presume that theatre is not Martin's thing after all the telly stuff. Though he hasn't done theatre for years he does have great capabilities as a classical actor. *Tartuffe* was something that he really wanted to do. He wanted a challenge.'

Lots of eyebrows were raised after the casting was announced but Martin reacted spiritedly. 'People say weird things to you when you work in the theatre, as if you're suddenly doing something that is akin to medicine, as opposed to television, which is akin to murder!' After 12 years' absence from the stage he said: 'I had a guilt thing about not doing theatre, which I didn't understand and don't approve of.'

The complex role was even harder than he had imagined, and Martin admitted afterwards: 'In the first fortnight of rehearsals I thought I had made a huge mistake and, if I say so now, they can get somebody else.' But Martin is not a quitter and he gritted his teeth and carried on.

The vast majority of the people who saw the play were delighted that he did so. The *Sunday Times* critic John Peter praised Martin's performance as 'wonderful' and spelled out why: 'When Martin Clunes appears, you'll know at once he is for real. Lie and truth coexist smugly in the big fleshy body. The professional hypocrite is someone who has resolved his own schizophrenia. Tartuffe is all frankness and confidence. There is nothing furtive, ingratiating or sanctimonious about him. ... This is one of the great Moliere performances. Clunes knows that such men are like compulsive gamblers: they have to be certain they will win. This performance is me. I believe in my role, therefore I am.'

But Toby Young in the *Spectator* could not have agreed less and slammed both the production and the star. He thought

Martin Clunes's performance was: 'Oddly subdued, as if the great privilege of appearing in a proper West End play was all a bit much for this low-brow television actor.'

The unhappy Mr Young sourly deemed the whole production 'unsophisticated' and concluded sourly: 'Clunes looks slightly uncomfortable in the role. Judging from this performance, his natural home is in panto.'

Although Martin's performance was widely acclaimed, he was not enamoured of the experience of performing at the National Theatre. In a feisty interview with the *Independent on Sunday* he spelled out the reasons why. 'I didn't really enjoy working at the National. I liked the people I worked with on the show, and I thought the production itself was great, but there's a sort of meanness of spirit in that building that I didn't like. On our last night, not a handshake, a glass of wine, a sausage roll, nothing. Then they charged me £11 a week just to park my car – and they own their own car park.'

He also criticised the snootiness of the National's audience. 'I didn't know what they were on about half the time,' he said. 'They came up to me and said things like, "It's good to see you are doing something worthwhile now." What does that mean? As if performing at the National is the only worthwhile thing you can do as an actor.'

A spokeswoman for the National Theatre said in sad response: 'I'm sorry that there were aspects of Martin's time at the National that he didn't enjoy. We enjoyed having him here, and the audience very much enjoyed seeing him as Tartuffe.'

CHAPTER 12

ACID AND CHIPS

*'All his victims considered him a friend — he should have
carried a government health warning'*
MARTIN CLUNES ON 'ACID BATH MURDERER'
JOHN GEORGE HAIGH

M artin had a hunch it was time that he played a
character with a real edge of villainy about him. He
was keen to stretch himself, so he was delighted to be asked
to play the infamous John George Haigh and bring back to
life one of life's most evil monsters.

It was the first time Martin had ever played a real-life
character and he joked: 'Playing a role like this, you can only
draw on personal experience. I do confess that I have not
actually murdered anyone, nor have I dissolved any dead
bodies in acid. But I think I have employed certain tricks and
charm that I have found successful on other people. Haigh
was a terrific charmer and conman.'

Martin had been working down in Cornwall, working on
a couple of films for Sky, when he received the script entitled
A is for Acid. On the cover was a picture of Haigh wearing a
Hannibal Lecter-style mask. Martin said later he thought:

'Now there's a contrast. Perhaps people who work in abattoirs look like that, but we never see them.' He knew Haigh would not be easy and that it would mean using 'acting muscles I hadn't used for a while'.

Haigh was a serial killer who was convicted of the murders of six people, although he confessed to killing at least three more. He was hanged at Wandsworth Prison in 1949. Ruthless Haigh believed, wrongly as it turned out, that he could carry out the perfect murder if he could completely destroy the bodies of his victims. His method was to dissolve the corpses in sulphuric acid and pour the remaining sludge down into the sewers. Then he stole his victims' money and valuables. But after his last victim, an elderly widow called Olive Durand-Deacon, was reported missing, the police found evidence of Haigh's evil activities.

Sludge still in Haigh's workshop was discovered to contain gallstones and a denture that were identified as belonging to the unfortunate Mrs Durand-Deacon. A jury quickly rejected Haigh's plea of insanity and he was sentenced to death.

Haigh is almost forgotten today and Martin noted that his generation knew hardly anything about the once feared villain. But he said his mother could remember the Haigh case very clearly as a dreadful event, adding, 'An older friend of mine said that he was often told as a child, "You eat that up or Haigh will get you!" He was a stock bogeyman of the day.'

Afterwards Martin told an interviewer that although the

murder scenes were 'horrible' to film, there were aspects of Haigh he could relate to. 'He was a bad engineer and I'm a bad carpenter. He wanted everyone to like him and I'm needy that way too. We are all curious about the human condition, and as an actor you explore things you wouldn't dream of doing in real life. You can't be squeamish as an actor.'

Haigh's bizarre mental outlook on life appeared to come from his fiercely religious parents, who had convinced him early on that he was one of God's chosen ones and therefore above the law, let alone any worries about morality. He was completely without conscience, which Martin conveyed quite brilliantly.

Martin knew he faced a massive uphill struggle to convey any humanity in Haigh but it was a challenge he was delighted to accept. What was particularly chilling about Haigh was that he murdered without malice. 'He had strong relationships with all his victims and he simply killed for profit. His victims were not chumps and they weren't taken in by a fool. All his victims considered him a friend – he should have carried a government health warning.'

This was a man behaving much worse than badly. Martin laughed that it was nice to play 'a moustache-twirling baddie'. He finds it relatively simple not to become too involved with his characters. 'You're not there to judge them or cure them, you're just there to inhabit them.' And he and director Harry Bradbeer set out to make Haigh look even more fiendish on screen than he must have been in real life.

They changed his favourite murder method from shooting to clubbing in order to emphasise the brutality of the man. Martin even smoked heavily as Haigh, although he pointed out 'they were herbal. I gave up real cigarettes two years ago because I want to meet my daughter's children.' Co-star Keeley Hawes, who played Haigh's innocent girlfriend Gillian, was greatly impressed by Martin's performance. 'Martin Clunes is an extraordinary actor, who has got a huge range and his portrayal of Haigh is mesmerising,' she said.

After the horrific Mr Haigh, Martin was more than happy to turn his hand to his complete opposite, a man who was the very epitome of kindness and consideration, and say hello to Mr Chips.

James Hilton's famous fictional schoolteacher, Mr Charles Chipping, would never have contemplated homicide even briefly. He was much too busy struggling against cruelty and unfairness and trying to bring the best out of his beloved pupils. Martin was very keen to take on the role after receiving a phone call from Nick Elliott, ITV's controller of drama. 'I didn't even read a script to be persuaded, though of course I pretended I did,' he said. 'In reality I was really keen on the project as soon as he mentioned it. It's not often an actor gets a chance to play the whole life of a character and that challenge attracted me instantly.'

Mr Chips might not have been a real person but along with Charles Dickens' Thomas Gradgrind and Muriel Spark's Jean Brodie he was a legendary teacher. Robert Donat first played Mr Chips in the 1939 film and won an

Oscar for his performance. Peter O'Toole revived the character 30 years later in a musical film version, with Petula Clark as his co-star.

The BBC then serialised *Goodbye Mr Chips* in six episodes in 1984, with Roy Marsden playing the charismatic teacher. The BBC had used Repton school in an attempt to recreate the fictional Brookfield School, which is said to be based on The Leys School, Cambridge, where James Hilton was a pupil during World War One. Martin and the ITV production team chose Winchester, which provided an equally convincing backdrop.

But Mr Chips had to age from 29 to 83 years during the story, which provided a stern challenge for the make-up department. It required specially crafted hooded eyes, a sequence of wigs, special milky contact lenses, false teeth with receding gums, false liver spots and a new nose.

The chief make-up artist Anne Spiers explained that Mr Chips was seen at four key stages in his life, in his late twenties, in his forties, in his sixties and in his eighties. 'Each of these four key different life stages had their own make-up effects. His middle age is 60 and, as people tend to age like their parents, Martin gave me a photo of his dad when he was about 55. So that was our starting point.'

Anne explained that it took three and a half hours to turn Martin into 83-year-old Mr Chips. 'But even ageing him to 60 took two and a half hours because it was more realistic to do it with paints than prosthetic pieces.'

The first job for the make-up department was to make a

plaster of Paris cast of Martin's head. 'We started with alginate, which is what dentists use to take moulds of people's teeth, and then applied the plaster of Paris. But we used far too much plaster which dragged his skin down – automatically ageing him. It was a complete accident, but a fortuitous one.'

Once the cast was finished, hundreds of photos were taken with Martin squinting his eyes and making a double chin just to see how his skin and flesh moved. Anne Spiers studied the cast carefully and drew on it to see what was popular with make-up. 'It was great,' she said. 'It sat on my kitchen table and I lived with it for weeks!'

Martin was on holiday when Anne started work, so at first she took the cast of his head around with her in the back of her car. 'I took it out with me under my arm to the wigmakers and to the people who create facial hair,' she said.

'We made prosthetics to give him a double chin and gave him a false nose because as you age your nose changes shape. It gets bigger and more grisly and the eyes begin to droop. We probably drooped them more than Martin's will in real life, but it's all artistic licence. We've tried to make him nice rather than scary or ugly!'

Martin happily admits he is not the most patient person in the world and he did not find it easy spending hours in make-up. 'I had to stop fidgeting,' he told *TV Times*. 'And that started me becoming like a real-life 83-year-old. I had to be more still, especially as, if it got hot, the prosthetics would just slide off my face because they were made with gelatine. But it was good not to be able to fidget or talk nonsense for a while. Everyone around me enjoyed the break too. Once the make-up was on, I instantly felt in character.'

It took so much to make Martin into an 83-year-old man that he found he couldn't just nip in and out of character. 'So I found I had to have a little lie down, just like a real old man,' he said. What he found fascinating was that members of the film unit – people he saw, laughed and joked with every day – started to want to take care of him. 'I'd feel a comforting arm around my back to help me along,' he explained. 'It was very, very tiring.'

But it did provide Martin with a somewhat disconcerting look in to the future. 'It's an odd sensation seeing myself look so old. It makes me think, "Bloody Hell! That's what it's going to be like in years to come." If I'm spared, that is.'

Martin loved the trappings of education back in Victorian times. 'When I put on Chipping's gown and mortarboard it gave me a feeling of power,' he said after filming had finished. 'You can see why schoolmasters used to favour them – it sets them apart from mere mortals. And we've been so lucky in that most of the filming has been done in real schools, including Harrow, Winchester and Douai Abbey School in Berkshire.'

Like most audiences, Martin adored Mr Chips but had to find quirks and faults in order to make the character interesting. 'He's a kindly man and a good teacher, but he is also a bit of a maverick and can be curmudgeonly. You suspect that his kindness is all rather calculated. He's a lone ship, sailing through the decades. I usually play horrible people like Gary from *Men Behaving Badly* with some chink in their armour… but Chips is so nice I've had to dig deep to find his weaknesses.'

Hilton is said to have written the original book in four days flat in 1933, which makes its enduring popularity all the more remarkable. Martin was nervous about whether his version would stand comparison with his illustrious predecessors. 'The alternative is too embarrassing to think about,' he said just after production. 'It's a case of wait and see. I have studiously kept away from the rushes and don't want to see it until it is finished.' He admitted to being 'frightened now I've done it. I'm frightened that it's OK. It's such a responsibility. It's such a great story, a national treasure. Both the previous Mr Chips films were pretty fantastic.'

The making of *Goodbye Mr Chips* was threatened in April 2002 when the government suddenly decided to scrap a tax break that benefited original television drama. Just as the £2million remake of the classic story was about to go into production the then Chancellor of the Exchequer, Gordon Brown, announced that the tax rules for film and television projects were to change. The benefits that producers gleaned from sale and leaseback arrangements which helped ease high costs during production were changed and it meant some swift refinancing.

Fortunately the prospect of Martin Clunes playing the legendary schoolmaster was too good for ITV to allow to founder for lack of money. The two-hour film was seen as a gem in the schedule and was already pencilled in as the big

Christmas attraction. *Goodbye Mr Chips* was transmitted on Boxing Day 2002 to rave reviews. The quality of the production and the sensitivity of Martin's performance were both widely praised.

Stuart Orme's deft direction chose a clear and unsentimental style that really registered with viewers. But it was Martin's portrayal of the eccentric yet effective Latin teacher that captivated the television audience. Martin said he was completely won over by the character. 'Mr Chips is special because of his decency,' he said. 'He's not superhuman, he's normal and that makes him all the more appealing.'

Mr Chipping arrives at Brookfield in the 1870s and his career almost ends on his first day after the headmaster discovers him struggling to control an unruly class. The grumpy head is all for sacking the new man but he is persuaded by German teacher Max Staefel to give him another chance. Mr Chippings is very grateful and his kindness is soon illustrated to the boys. When he finds one youngster has lost a halfpenny belonging to a senior boy he quietly recompenses him and advises more care in future.

The caring teacher quickly learns to control unruly classes and Martin allowed him a delicious secret smile after he has quelled a would-be troublemaker by a spot of public ridicule. He hates to have to deliver the cane and always prefers to administer his own brand of verbal justice, accompanied by detention and lines.

On a lonely walking holiday Mr Chippings meets the charmingly dotty Kathie, played by Victoria Hamilton, and gallantly saves her from a soaking as she overreaches herself on the branch of a tree. Love blossoms with captivating innocence and Kathie renames her new husband Mr Chips. She encourages him to believe that teaching is 'terribly important' and he becomes re-enthused over his profession.

Tragedy strikes when Kathie dies in childbirth along with their baby son. Mr Chips is mortified and there is more gloom ahead. A new headmaster is keen on establishing army training and putting the fees up. It seems the old standards revered by Mr Chips are under threat but the whole school is behind him and the new head and his radical ideas of economies are swiftly shown the door. Mr Chips is asked to take over as the new head and when a German aircraft bombs the school he shows his formidable courage.

Mr Chips stays on after World War One and dies happy in his beloved school when he is well into his eighties. (Martin's exhaustive make-up sessions stand up to the challenge very well). One of the most memorable scenes is when Chips reads a list of the pupils killed in action. For everyone else they are just names, but for Chips each name has a face attached. As he finally dies the doctor says how sad it is that he never had children. Chips overhears and says he had children, 'hundreds of them... all boys.'

The production was a success all over the world. The *Los Angeles Times* said: 'Martin Clunes does a fine job playing Chips through the years, and in the end is suitably heroic, embodying as he does what must be the nearly universal hope that in the end all our unspectacular life's work ultimately will be appreciated as the great gift it is.'

Martin was finding himself in great demand and in that happy situation all actors dream of where they can choose which roles they want to undertake. Martin's next choice was heartfelt, though a little bizarre. He decided to accept the offer of a role in an animated adaptation of the children's favourite Fungus the Bogeyman. He joked that he would have been happy to play the title role without make-up but 'unfortunately they were sold on doing the computer version.'

In fact Martin played a human called George who wants to capture a Bogeyman and expose him to the world. Martin insisted his character was not such an evil guy. 'George is all right. He's hapless with bad sweater but he is a good sort. He just thinks it might help him with his career. He is a not very successful journalist on a not particularly important local newspaper and he thinks capturing a Bogeyman could be his big break.'

Martin was happy to play the role because he had loved Raymond Briggs' stories as a child. 'I remember when the book came out there was all this controversy about should we be leading our kids astray with stories about slime and foul things and all that nonsense. But they're what children love. I certainly did!'

CHAPTER 13

UNDERTAKING WILLIAM AND MARY

*'It's strange that I had to wait until my forties to act as a dad.
I know how parenthood changes your attitudes to life'*
MARTIN CLUNES

O n the surface, playing a shy and lonely undertaker searching for a lover through the lonely hearts section of the internet doesn't seem like the most promising platform for hilarious comedy. But Martin recognised top quality comic potential the moment he read the very first script of *William and Mary*.

Original ideas are often thin on the ground in an area where executives are reluctant to take a chance. But Martin knew that writer Mick Ford had come up with an exceptional new series. 'I recognised right away that the scripts were extremely good, with three dimensional characters and a great story,' he said.

The sensitive six-part romantic drama *William and Mary* was an ambitious project for ITV1, with a great deal depending on the screen chemistry between Martin as widower undertaker William Shawcross and Julie Graham as divorced midwife Mary Gilchrist.

William has been left bringing up two spirited young teenage daughters after his wife had been killed in a motoring accident. Mary's feckless husband has left her caring for their two sons. Mary lives in an inner-city council flat while William is comparatively wealthy and has a smart house in one of the better suburbs. The story starts with William poring over pictures of available young women on his computer and after he picks out beautiful Mary he quickly becomes captivated.

'Mary is cautiously prepared to give it a go if she finds the right man,' said Martin. 'The question is, "Is William that fella?" The first date is by no means a galloping success but there is obviously an attraction between them. It is all very honest, with moments of deep poignancy and others that are very funny, which is what middle-aged love is all about, it seems to me.'

That first date has some awkward moments and is interrupted by a call to a complicated pregnancy back at the hospital. The second time around things go better and there is an instant earthy attraction between the characters and they are soon sharing steamy sessions, including a memorable liaison in a hotel bathtub. Julie said later that however realistic it appeared on screen, 'he had underwear on and so did I. It wasn't embarrassing at all. It was just fun.'

Martin was quick to agree. 'I showed my bum in the film *Staggered* and the TV film *Dirty Tricks*, and I think that is enough for the British public. This time around, I asked the producers, "Do you mind if I don't show my bum?" because

I don't want to become the bum guy. It seems to have cropped up a lot. It's not quite the opening in television I was looking for!'

Martin was extra-sensitive about his shape at the time because after giving up smoking he had put on quite a lot of weight. 'I didn't want my bum to be shown because it's racing down my legs,' he said frankly. 'Now I've bought some running shoes and I'm determined to sort it out.'

Martin had already had an on-screen fling with Julie in *Dirty Tricks*, which helped the love scenes to look very natural, and each actor paid tribute to the other. 'If you make it awkward it can be awkward, but with Martin we just know each other so well it wasn't a problem,' said Julie.

There was a lot of joking between the two stars and Julie even bought Martin a 'fart machine' that she placed inside a coffin during one deeply serious scene. 'It was Martin's birthday during the shoot,' Julie recalled, 'and I didn't know what to get him because he's already got everything. The machine was a little box with a remote control and it could make five different farting noises. I stood at the back of the crematorium setting it off. He wasn't too impressed!'

The nature of the series is that real life just keeps getting in the way of the path of true love. Mary is shattered when a patient suddenly dies and then shocked when the undertaker turns out to be none other than her new lover, who has been somewhat economical with the truth of his real profession because of his concern that dating an undertaker would not exactly be a turn-on for any young woman.

Martin explained later that what really appealed most to him about the series was that while he didn't know anything about undertaking, he had recently learned a little about midwifery when his daughter was born. 'And as it was written by a man I thought, "My God, he must really know that I've been through all this."

'It was written by someone who had really experienced becoming a father rather than just by someone who had been through a book looking for info on it. It was all told from an intensely personal point of view. I found out that the writer, Mick Ford, had a large family and he has been through these battles of having teenagers and so on. That just made the whole thing sort of ring home.'

Julie believed in the show from the start and said it was unlike anything else on television. 'It's not a medical drama. It's not a police drama. No one gets killed, maimed or raped. It's just a funny drama about two people who should be together.'

Martin particularly appreciated the way that both humour and drama came naturally out of the situation. 'It was clever writing,' he said. 'The prime raw material is the script. It is so important. Actors sometimes think that if you say lines quickly enough audiences won't notice if it's sub-standard, or if they fall over that'll be funny. But this stuff was really engaging and interesting and as the scripts came in, each one had a massive surprise that you'd never seen coming and that has been true throughout.'

Having played lovers before clearly helped the stars. Julie said they had previously had to do very graphic sex scenes for about a week. 'We'd already seen each other's bits,' she laughed. Julie pointed out that with some scripts featuring love affairs, the participants have to 'manufacture' the relationship but it just developed between the characters on *William and Mary*. 'In fact, quite a few times we were told off for getting on too well. We knew what was coming but we had to be warned not to get ahead of the script.'

It was the first series on television in which Martin had played a father. 'I felt that it was very strange that I had to wait until my forties to act as a dad,' he said. 'I know how parenthood changes your attitudes to life. Ever since Emily was born four years ago I have become fascinated by programmes that feature parents. Stories where a child is in peril cease to be about that annoying brat. Suddenly as a parent you can't but feel that your heart is right with them.'

Being a parent helped him play the role convincingly, he said. But Emily was only three or four at the time the series was made and, as Martin said, William was the father of teenage girls. 'We were about to do another scene of shouting and bitching with the girls when I said to our director, "It seems like this is all we do." And she said, very down to earth, "Yes, they're teenage girls, that is what happens." So I suppose I have got all that to come.'

Martin recognised early on that both William and Mary were both 'slightly damaged goods', but understood perfectly why they would go to a dating agency to find a new relationship. He felt it was an entirely natural way to behave in the modern world. 'If you're very busy the chances of meeting a new partner are very limited,' he said. 'Lots of people do to go to a dating agency, and I think it requires amazing courage and is not at all an admission of defeat. It's just a practical necessity sort of thing and a clever way of going about it. William and Mary are both practical people. They realise that in their jobs they only meet infants and dead people.' But the characters have a great deal in common. 'They are both bringing up children single-handedly and they are both very romantic,' said Martin.

The co-stars shared a similar sense of humour which helped to make the production a happy one. 'At least she laughs at all my stupid jokes and it is just easy working together,' said Martin. 'It's hard not to sound ghastly like actors gushing together but it is great to have nothing in the way. We don't need to cover for each other. We were told off at the end of the second series for kissing too often. They had to throw water over us once like a couple of old dogs!'

But beneath the laughter the actors always took great care with the more sensitive scenes. 'Sensitivity goes with the role when you play an undertaker,' said Martin. 'I've learned a lot about a very difficult and vital job. I haven't had to embalm anyone or put them into a coffin or anything like that but I've taken on board lots of little things, like the way undertakers don't wear their gloves – they carry them. I have learned an awful lot about the profession and I have learned to admire them. It is interesting to me. Undertakers are right next to all of us. Every small town has an undertaker's catering for their community, and it is a business that is never going to go away.'

Not surprisingly his character's profession provoked thoughts about Martin's own mortality more than once, and he revealed one decision made during filming. Much of the filming took place in Wimbledon near where Martin grew up. 'We filmed at Putney Vale Crematorium, where my father was cremated,' he said. 'I had a look in one of the ovens.' And that gave him real food for thought. 'I don't want to be cremated,' he said emphatically.

Martin was alarmed to learn that not everything breaks down in the burning process and afterwards they put all the remains through a crushing machine with ball bearings. It helped Martin to decide that he definitely did not fancy being burned. 'Who knows if you don't still feel things?' he told a reporter. 'It would really hurt, wouldn't it? I think I would rather take my chances with the worms. It seems a more natural, mulchy way out. Maybe it's cowardice.'

There were other real-life echoes in the script. His mother Daphne still lived in Wimbledon at the time, and when William's mother dies in the story, the producers staged her funeral in St Mary's Church, Wimbledon. This was the same church where Martin's father's funeral had been held and where his sister had got married.

Martin could not resist making a jokey invitation and called his real mother and said, 'Do you want to come to your funeral?' 'And she did,' said Martin. Sadly she did not quite make it onto the screen. 'You don't see her in the programme. There was a long shot of the mourners, but the camera clicked off just before it got to her.'

Martin was even asked to address a real undertakers' convention, but he was a little too daunted to accept. 'I don't know the subject that well and I'm not a big public speaker anyway,' he said. Martin tends to ration public appearances to his charity work, but the importance of the undertaker's job did impress him. As he said after production: 'To catch people in freefall at perhaps the most difficult and distressing moment in their lives takes some considerable tact and skill.

'I can remember when my father died and the undertaker came round. There was a load of things my mother had to do. And that helped to bring some order out of the chaos. "What kind of casket?" "What handles?" "What time?" Those were all questions she had to address and it just gave some structure to the worst experience she had ever had happen to her. The funeral gives a vital punctuation to the grieving process. After the undertaker has done his job, hopefully you're ready to continue your grieving on your own. With Julie's character bringing babies into the world and mine seeing them out of it, we completed the circle.'

Viewers loved the show and ITV recorded some of the highest audience appreciation figures for a homemade drama serial. But the critics were mixed to say the least. The *Guardian* described Mick Ford's script as 'smart, charming and deft' and went on to enthuse that the show was 'immediately engaging, fluid and funny, and most of the characters were well-rounded and genuine, and its premise was the feelgood stuff of cosy nights in.'

But the paper's reviewer, Gareth McLean, refused to accept

the idea of Martin Clunes playing Mr Nice Guy. He said: 'Unfortunately, all of this was overshadowed by the monumental miscasting of Martin Clunes as William and Julie Graham as Mary. While he has lately been attempting to be more of a grown-up – most recently in *Goodbye, Mr Chips* – *Men Behaving Badly* is not yet a distant enough memory for Clunes to convince as a slightly square widower and father-of-two. The image of seed-soaked tissues stuck to his face is a difficult one to dislodge from one's brain.' He went on to blast Julie Graham for having 'plenty of sass but no sincerity'.

Martin and ITV were happy to discover that the gentle series survived the criticism to become a popular hit. It took a while, but as the first run came to an end, Claire Stoker said in the *Liverpool Echo*: 'This drawn-out romantic drama finally came to a close with Martin Clunes proving he has what it takes to carry a series... Clunes is rapidly turning into a national treasure and proving he is capable of so much more than *Men Behaving Badly*.

'Following in the footsteps of John Thaw and David Jason, it can only be a matter of time before he lands a role as a curmudgeonly detective.'

Clearly ITV bosses agreed with Miss Stoker's assessment. In May 2003 drama controller Nick Elliott announced that, after averaging audiences of 8.1 million, *William and Mary* would see a second series go into production later in the year.

The ebullient Elliott is a great fan of Martin's work and he swiftly followed that up with another commission for the actor. A six-part series called *Doc Martin* – to be loosely based on the character Martin had played in the Brenda Blethyn film *Saving Grace* – was to be made by Buffalo Productions.

Martin was delighted that ITV wanted his wife Philippa to produce, but he was slightly less enchanted when Nick Elliott enthused that he was 'the David Jason of the next 20 years'. Martin wondered privately if the actual David Jason might be a little miffed as he was very much still around but he wisely said nothing and smiled.

In fact Martin got the chance to ring the changes of his TV identity in September 2003 as he starred with Neil Pearson in a lively little TV movie called *The Booze Cruise* which was a comic romp across the channel to buy cheap drink. Unfortunately a leaden script made the one-off comedy something of an ordeal for actors and viewers alike. The jokes were desperately predictable, but the performances were creditable as all concerned tried to inject as much amusement as possible into a sub-standard script. With Mark Benton and Brian Murphy in a high quality cast they just about made it watchable.

For one young waitress working in a coastal hotel, however, meeting the production team provided a memorable end to a difficult day. Fiona Cook posted a tribute on Martin's charity website and said: 'Martin Clunes is a top bloke who, seeing that I'd had the day from hell at work, bought me a drink and invited me to join him and Neil Pearson and a group of people he was filming with. I've never forgotten how sweet he was.'

Martin played a middle-aged businessman called Clive

with a terrible taste in sweaters who got spectacularly car sick almost before the journey had got going. 'I had to age up to play him,' said Martin, 'so I had grey streaks in my hair, a false moustache which was very tickly and an awful apricot jumper. As soon as we'd finished filming I couldn't wait to get rid of the disastrous jumper and moustache.'

Clive was a successful businessman who sails over to France with three of his neighbours and his prospective son-in-law to stock up on cheap alcohol. 'I can't see the attraction of a booze cruise myself,' Martin admitted. 'I am happy to travel for all sorts of reasons but booze is not one of them. The only thing I bought for real when we were in the French hypermarket was some tobacco for my accountant.

'But there's always something interesting about people going on a journey together. This trip certainly doesn't turn out to be the jolly outing they had hoped it would be. Clive wants to buy champagne for his daughter's wedding but none of the men has much in common and the trouble starts pretty much as soon as they set off.'

Most of the comedy came from Brian Murphy as xenophobic Maurice, who insisted the French lost the Battle of Waterloo because Napoleon was laid up with haemorrhoids. The best joke came when moaning Maurice dozed off and had sun block applied to his bald head to leave the word 'tit' branded on it. Overall the end result was less than memorable but the romp attracted an impressive viewing audience of over nine million and a sequel was swiftly commissioned.

Martin was clearly in great demand. When the BBC started trying out guest presenters to replace the axed Angus Deayton on the satirical quiz show *Have I Got News For You*, his name quickly came up. Martin's trial show was screened on 25 April 2003 and he was so good he quickly became one of the favourites to land the role of presenter permanently. There was much ill-founded newspaper speculation and the BBC put out a statement insisting the reports were 'premature'. A BBC spokesman said: Martin Clunes is one of several guest presenters we have had and no decision has been made on who will permanently fill the slot. A decision will be made sometime in the summer.'

In the event, as ratings for the 'auditions' shows remained higher than when Deayton had been in charge, the BBC decided not to have a permanent host and to continue changing presenters for each show. 'It's worked so well for us this way that we're going to continue with it,' said Lorraine Heggessey, controller of BBC1. 'It's clear audiences like different presenters. It fosters more interest and excitement.'

Heggessey had been particularly impressed by Martin's performance, but the two team captains, Ian Hislop and Paul Merton, were happy not to have a fixed replacement for Deayton. Hislop generously noted, however, that: 'Martin was great when he did the show.'

By the time the cast and crew had reconvened for the second series of *William and Mary*, Martin's co-star Julie Graham was pregnant and her emotions often got the better

Martin in 2005,
promoting series 3 of
William and Mary.

Above left: Martin relaxing at the 2006 Chelsea Flower Show.

Above right: Making new friends and judging a dog show in Dorset, where Martin and Philippa live with their daughter, Emily.

Below: Martin appearing as a policeman in a performance to celebrate the Queen's 80th birthday.

'Doc Martin' becomes a real doctor as Martin receives an honorary doctorate
from Bournemouth University in 2007.

Above left: Martin is keen to get involved with local events – here, he is pictured at a fun day at Milton Abbey school in Dorset.

Above right: On location in Australia for *Martin Clunes: A Man and his Dogs*.

Below left and right: Martin with his beloved dogs, Tina, Arthur and Mary.

Above left: Martin meets a new friend at a signing for his book *A Dog's Life* in 2008.

Above right: Looking relaxed at the 2008 Chelsea Flower Show.

Below: Martin appearing on *Friday Night with Jonathan Ross*.

Above: Martin and Philippa enjoying the Royal Windsor Horse Show.

Below left: Martin signs a copy of his book at a fundraising event in Dorset.

Below right: Showing his support for the Born Free Foundation in 2009.

Above and below left: Launching the Born Free Foundation's 'Wild and Live' event, celebrating 25 years of the Foundation's work with endangered animals.

Below right: Martin with Great Britain's champion showjumper Ellen Whitaker at the 2009 Horse of the Year Show.

Martin Clunes is undoubtedly one of the country's favourite stars, and with a host of future projects planned his continued success is assured for years to come.

of her. 'Julie would cry at the drop of a hat,' said Martin. 'And if I saw her upset then it would upset me. I cry easily!'

The emotional nature of the show left a huge impression on Martin, who said he was proud to be involved with such an appealing love story. 'I know it sounds a bit naff, but I am a romantic and, doing a love story as real as this one, you do get swept away, or at least I do.'

The second series begins with the couple celebrating their engagement and starting to make wedding plans. But all preparations are thrown up in the air when Mary tells William she is pregnant with his baby. William is immediately overwhelmed with emotion – and so was Martin. 'I found myself welling up with tears during the scene where William has been at choir practice,' said the actor. 'Julie really was pregnant so that made the news even more exciting. But I also remembered the lovely situation of when my wife Philippa told me I was going to be a dad and I drew on that experience for the scene.'

All the way through Martin was able to use real life parallels to convey a scene more convincingly and make William more believable. When the wedding scenes came, Martin even made sure he had not seen her dress in advance so his reaction would be all the more authentic. 'The scene reminded me so much of my own wedding,' he said. 'I hadn't seen Philippa's dress until she walked in on her father's arm.'

On a less happy note Martin took time out at the launch of the second series to berate a journalist who had suggested that the love scenes with Julie looked so convincing there must be something going on between the two. 'She sort of insinuated that nobody is that good at acting!' said Martin, who was furious because there was no truth to it whatsoever. 'It was good acting. Neither of us is cheating on our partners. Yes, we have got a great chemistry between us as we have worked together before. We like each other enormously and I can't think of an actress who I respect as much as Julie. I think she is the perfect acting machine. She is honest, truthful and unusual. That hack has insulted both of us.'

Before work began on the third series of *William and Mary* the Clunes family took a holiday in their beloved Maldives. Martin was refreshed and eager to get back to work, but talking to the young actresses who play William's daughters made him worry about the day his own daughter Emily would be ready for relationships. 'I just can't bear thinking about Emily having boyfriends,' he smiled to an interviewer. 'Peta Cornish, who plays one of my daughters in the series, is going off to South America to do a trek. I'm not even going to tell Emily there is a South America! Dear God, no – that would be awful. I'm forbidding boyfriends and I am sure I won't be nearly as nice as William is about it.'

By series three William and Mary have a 20-month old baby, Thomas, and their relationship has really moved on. But in a dramatic twist Mary starts to suspect that William is being unfaithful to her and has found another woman. 'William does not have an affair,' said Martin, keen to defend the undertaker's character. 'The woman in question is his cousin's widow, but William comes home smelling of her perfume and the mistrust builds.'

Although *William and Mary* remained popular with the viewers, the show frequently attracted criticism for its feel-good approach to life. But Martin strongly defended the series. 'Birth and death are huge grand opera subjects,' he said. 'They affect us all and they are what are really important. Add the pressures of work and education fuelling things at home and you can see that *William and Mary* is about issues that affect everyone. This show doesn't exclude anyone.'

The serial was also sometimes criticised for a lack of 'gritty realism' but Martin insisted that the serial never pulled its punches. 'I think there's a move away from dead prostitute programmes, though I am sure there will always be a market for them. But I think *Cold Feet* started a move back towards dramas about things that really affect us, and we are continuing that.'

CHAPTER 14

THE MAN WHO ALMOST LOST HIS NOSE

'I was promised the spirits wouldn't be cross with me'
MARTIN ON HIS UNWITTING TRANSGRESSION OF TRADITION BY
CHEWING GUM IN A MAORI MEETING HOUSE

Although Martin was fully aware that the extraordinary international success of *Men Behaving Badly* meant that he was known in 50 countries around the globe, it still came as something of a surprise when he first set foot in New Zealand to find his face was familiar to the Kiwi population at large.

In the week Martin flew into Auckland to prepare for a starring role in a new comedy drama called *The Man Who Lost His Head*, New Zealand TV just happened to be showing eight hours of *Doc Martin* in a row. *William and Mary* had also been favourably received when screened in the land of the long white cloud, and Martin found it quite strange to be known in another country so far from the UK. It was another reminder of just how far the tentacles of television travel.

The Man Who Lost His Head was an unusual light-hearted project in that it had a cast that consisted mainly of Maoris. Martin had been in on the project right from the treatment stage, and from the start he had been attracted to the prospect of playing a character who was a real fish out of water. And the thought of working in New Zealand for six weeks, he admitted, had him signing on the dotted line immediately. It was a country he had never visited.

The role was that of Ian Bennet, a seriously studious curator from the British Imperial Museum who is about to marry his boss's nice but bossy daughter. He then finds his life turned upside down when he is sent to the other side of the world with a difficult mission for a man with limited experiences of life.

His task is to politely decline Maori claims for the return by Britain of a carved wooden head of a Maori chief to the small fictional New Zealand town of Otakataka. Awaiting his arrival in New Zealand is a very determined Maori group but, after initial frosty confrontations, the curator finds himself drawn to their community, their ways, their rights – and one woman in particular.

Martin's introduction to New Zealand did not get off to the best of starts. His plane landed half an hour late, and after he had reclaimed his luggage he found that the car booked to collect him and his family from the airport was nowhere to be found. Martin presumed that the driver must have got fed up with waiting and driven off. It was an inconvenience, but he decided this was probably the kind of laid-back Kiwi attitude he would have to get used to.

Despite this hiccup, Martin arrived in New Zealand in extremely good heart. The country is made up of two islands and, as a confirmed island-lover, he was looking forward eagerly to exploring them both. He was also feeling reinvigorated after spending ten days holiday in Mexico and California with Philippa and Emily, and he was so pleased that they had been able to fly on to New Zealand with him. With *The Man Who Lost His Head* not scheduled to begin shooting for a few days, there was a chance to spend some time as a family enjoying the hospitality and the sights of a country that was new to all of them.

They found the New Zealanders they met welcoming and genuinely friendly, and Martin was instantly smitten with the country. Its sheer geographical beauty took his breath away.

Filming was due to take place on the west coast of North Island near Auckland, so it made sense to head for South Island and its coasts, which otherwise they might not have had a chance to see. 'We went to all the places which looked quite Cornish,' Martin said, 'including Raglan, a small surfing town that's really rather hippyish. So it was a bit like being in *Doc Martin*, but with more reggae.'

A highlight was a helicopter trip from Nelson to Kaikoura, one of the most strikingly beautiful towns on the east coast of South Island, situated about 110 miles north of Christchurch. Here the mountains stretch down not far from the sea, and the waters off Kaikoura are famous for their abundance of marine life. The family jumped at the chance to go out on a boat on a whale-watching excursion and to their delight they sighted not just whales but large pods of leaping, frolicking bottle-nose dolphins, an albatross and a colony of seals.

Before he set foot on New Zealand soil Martin was by his

own admission ignorant of all things Maori. It was a conscious decision on his part not to immerse himself in Maori history and its traditions but to learn as he went along. He viewed the story of *The Man Who Lost His Head* as a journey of discovery and resolved to make the same journey as the unworldly Ian Bennet. 'I was attracted to the idea of my character being a fish out of water and I could relate to his ignorance of the Maori culture,' he explained.

Once in the country, Martin swiftly learned something of the culture when the cast and crew had a traditional Maori blessing, not just before the start of filming but even before the read-through. The blessing was the first of several which ensued as filming progressed. Maori advisers were assigned to the production every step of the way to ensure authenticity and accurate representation. Before a funeral scene could be shot, a song and prayer was required to be offered up. 'Everything had to be squared with the gods,' Martin observed.

For Martin, some aspects of Maori life took some getting used to. 'The hakas, the greetings, are all quite in your face,' he noted, 'and people stick their tongues out at you. Then you press noses with people so that you breathe the same air. The idea is that it puts you on a level playing field with people.'

Most of the central cast were Maoris, and Martin soon won them over by refusing to demand a special trailer on location or request any sort of preferential treatment. Martin is not one for throwing his considerable weight about anyway, but this was most definitely one production where any big star behaviour would have been right out of place.

THE MAN WHO ALMOST LOST HIS NOSE

The only blemish in Martin's respect for Maori traditions occurred when it came to understanding the customs and rituals to be adhered to in a Maori meeting place known as a *marae*. Such Maori etiquette dictates no eating, no sitting on a table and no wearing of shoes, but Martin accidentally broke the rules by chewing gum and wearing shoes. When he subsequently suffered a painful accident and ended up on the floor with blood pouring from his nose, there were some knowing glances and sage nodding of heads that this was divine retribution for his transgression.

'We were filming a scene where a carved head is being thrown around the *marae*,' recalled Martin. 'I'd been using a rubber head for rehearsals and didn't take in the fact that it was later switched for a wooden one. I took it on the conk and it was actually quite painful. You could hear the crack when the carving hit my nose. It cut it and made it bleed and I was in agony for hours afterwards.'

The carving had struck Martin right across the bridge of his nose. It had been hurled at him at some considerable speed and he counted himself lucky it did not strike him any higher on his face or the impact could have taken his eye out.

Emergency repairs were needed, however, and this was effected by means of some new plastic skin created to cover the injury for the sake of continuity. Fortunately the make-up designer managed to disguise the injury enough to ensure filming was not interrupted in any major way and happily no lasting damage was done. Martin was also suitably contrite for having unwittingly flouted Maori traditions. 'I was promised that the spirits wouldn't be cross with me because I was a welcome influence bringing fun,' he said with some relief.

The accident happened on the day that Martin had set aside plenty of time after filming to accompany Philippa and Emily to the airport to see them off back to England. The delay for running repairs to his face ate into the allotted time and ultimately meant a dash to the airport as soon as the scene was completed.

On reflection, Martin felt that it was possibly for the best, as he was dreading shedding tears in front of Emily and Philippa at the departure gate. In the scramble to make sure they caught their flight there was little time to think about how much he was going to miss them once they were back home 11,500 miles away. Ahead of him were four further weeks in New Zealand and on the way back from the airport, he was feeling so bereft and thinking of them so much that he missed his turning off the freeway three times and had to double back each time.

The remainder of the shoot progressed smoothly, apart from one moment when Martin was unceremoniously unseated by a horse in a scene that called for him to ride bareback. Martin was no stranger to sitting astride a horse and his white mount, called Shadow, was experienced in the ways of filming, having appeared in *Xena the Warrior Princess* and *Hercules*. It should therefore have been a trouble-free partnership between horse and rider. 'But he picked up on the language on set,' said Martin, 'and when the word "Action!" was shouted he got excited and ready to go.

'I had no saddle or stirrup and the horse just bucked and

unseated me. I was flipped off and found myself standing next to him. Luckily the wrangler had kept a hold on him. He was a lovely horse and we actually got on well together because I had been for an incredible two-hour ride on him with my family.'

On that occasion Martin, Philippa and Emily, by now seven years old, had ridden along the pristine sandy shore at Bethells Beach, a beautiful secluded stretch of coastline approximately 20 miles north west of Auckland at the mouth of the Waitakere River where it flows into the Tasman Sea. Then they rode up into the hills beyond before picking their way through undergrowth into an untouched bush wilderness devoid of any tracks or trails.

It was especially exhilarating for the family because it was the first time the three of them had experienced horseback thrills together. Martin and Philippa had each learned to ride when they were small and Emily had been riding since she was two, first sitting on Shetland ponies in Richmond Park. This particular ride proved to be such a rewarding experience for Martin that it rekindled his interest in riding and he resolved to acquire his own horse once he had returned home.

Some of the filming took place in Little Huia, a small, out of the way community in an area of breathtaking scenery with strong connections to pioneer settler history on Auckland's Wild West Coast. But all the fun sequences of the drama were shot on Bethells Beach. Martin revelled in the area's natural beauty and when shooting finished, he strode across the sand and took one last dip in the sea as his own personal way of saying goodbye.

Martin spent six weeks on location in New Zealand but filming commitments were so tight that he was only able to take one full weekend off during that time. He therefore was unable to see as much of the country as he would have wished.

Nevertheless, working and staying in New Zealand, he could reflect, had provided many pleasant experiences, not least how much of a coffee drinker he had become after always being by choice more of a tea drinker. Martin found that New Zealanders took their coffee very seriously so that even the machine on set dispensed good cups of espresso.

New Zealand also dealt him one major surprise which left Martin shaking in his shoes – literally. In Auckland, he stayed at a luxury hotel called Mollies, situated in the inner city suburb of St. Mary's Bay and overlooking the city harbour. One evening Martin was in his room when he was alarmed to feel it starting to shake quite considerably. When the room stopped shuddering, it was followed by an unsettling silence all around.

Martin dismissed it as probably just a bit of a tremor, only to discover from the newspapers the following day that he had experienced the biggest earthquake in the area in 30 years.

As much as he had enjoyed his time in New Zealand, marvelled at its spectacular scenery, met some fascinating people and made some lasting friendships, by the end of six weeks of filming Martin was looking forward to going back to England. He had missed his family dreadfully and wanted to see 'my girls' again – and the new home in Dorset into which they were due to move in three weeks' time.

CHAPTER 15

LOSING IT

*'Most of us are astonishingly ignorant of what
cancer means and what it does'*
MARTIN CLUNES

Martin Clunes is one of those actors who always welcomes a new challenge. So when he was offered a part in a new comedy drama called *Losing It*, about the improbable subject for hilarity of testicular cancer, he accepted the role right away.

With his father's death from cancer never far from the back of his mind, Martin was more than happy to take on anything that would highlight the dangers of the disease in such an easily accessible way. 'As soon as I read the script, I wanted to do it,' he said. 'Not least because it is a drama which all men should heed. Sadly, men are more than a bit stupid when it comes to their health – they think things will just go away. They convince themselves that it will disappear and it doesn't. So I hope that *Losing It* will make them take notice.'

The writer of *Losing It* was Paul Mendelson, who had himself been diagnosed with testicular cancer in 1989. At the time he was working as the head of a creative department of an advertising agency. He was approaching 40 and worried that he was getting too old to keep winning at a young man's game.

Mendelson was determined to use humour to help him get over the experience. After his operation to remove the diseased testicle he placed a walnut on the desk of each of his colleagues when he returned to work. 'I said it was "a present from my holiday",' said Mendelson. 'They realised that if I could joke about the situation, they could too.'

His script, which was originally for a radio play, drew heavily on those deeply frightening real-life experiences and adopted the same dark and uncompromising sense of humour. The writing rang true with Martin – it was the main reason he accepted the role – and the humour was essential to him. 'If you make something too dark people tend to switch off,' he said. 'We wanted to deal with a serious subject in a light-hearted way. We wanted people who had switched on at the beginning to still be there at the end.'

His character, advertising copywriter Phil MacNaughton, is quite a worrier all round. 'He worries about his job and he's a hypochondriac,' explained Martin. 'Then he's diagnosed with cancer and he's really scared. He has a problem sharing his fear with his family because he's trying to protect them in a way. He thinks it's only happening to him, when of course it's having a huge impact on them as well.

'The humour doesn't stop, though. They are quite a funny family in the normal course of events, and it carries on even after the cancer diagnosis. This drama is not maudlin or gloomy. It's filled with hope and light.

'Of course my life has been touched by this terrible disease,' he continued. 'I've had friends and family who have been affected. But then, which of us hasn't, in some way, been affected at some point in our lives?

'I actually went to a close mate of mine who had been through breast cancer not so long ago, and I questioned her very hard about how she'd felt, what she went through and what issues it raised. Most of us are astonishingly ignorant of what cancer means – and what it does.'

For research, Martin took advice supplied by Cancer Research UK, which was involved throughout. He also spoke at length to Paul Mendelson and to cancer experts and patients to establish how his character would be feeling. 'We devised a points system while we were shooting,' he said, 'so I'd know how tired or sore my character would be at any particular time. We talked to people about their treatment.

'Being in the radiotherapy room was harrowing. One thing my friend said was that you feel a bit lonely and sorry for yourself in the treatment room because you are tired, worn down, and you are in there on your own. The nursing staff has to be in another room, and talk to you through a speaker.'

By the end of production Martin had become close to Mendelson. 'It was handy,' Martin deadpanned. 'If I had a question, Paul had the answer. I didn't need to find one-bollocked men!'

Losing It was not the first time that a popular celebrity had been used to bring the testicular cancer message home to men. In 1999 Everyman, a campaign organised by the Institute of Cancer Research to target male cancers, had brought in singer Robbie Williams to reach men between 20 and 35, who are most likely to be affected by the disease.

Martin had been alarmed to learn that testicular cancer was on the rise – its incidence had doubled in the previous 20 years. He was very keen to point out the positive message in the programme. 'The point is that, at any age, testicular cancer is one of the most treatable diseases. About 99 per cent of sufferers can be cured if they're caught early enough and, even when the tumour has spread it can still be cured in 95 per cent of cases. One of the things I loved about *Losing It* was that here is a character who has cancer and doesn't die. There are plenty of jokes. It is not called a one-off drama for nothing. The message is basically optimistic.'

He was quick to insist, however, that *Losing It* was not made as a campaigning film. 'It's a drama that is there to tell a story. But if one bloke with a lump in his balls feels moved to go to the doctor's as a result, it will be a good day's work.

'One of the reasons I wanted to take this part was because the story shows that family life does go on even after a cancer diagnosis. Another motivation was because I don't remember seeing testicular cancer in a television drama. Somebody watching it will have had the diagnosis that day. This drama shows that people who get cancer don't all die. Lots of people think they do. I really hope this programme will make people more aware of this particular type of cancer.'

Holly Aird, who played the wife of Martin's character, was quick to testify to the good cheer that prevailed in the production. 'It wasn't depressing on set,' she said. 'We didn't sit around talking about death all the time. There were lots of laughs. The script made me realise how hard it must be for the partner of the cancer victim – how you have to keep your head up and support everyone.'

Martin particularly liked the way the story has a lack of heroism. 'It is more about my character's selfishness of keeping everything to himself for so long and the impact it has on his family.' But some scenes were tough. 'I actually felt alone and isolated when we shot the scenes in the chemotherapy unit. I felt very vulnerable, very sad and a bit weepy. It was completely harrowing. And I was just acting and the machine wasn't even switched on.'

It was not an easy role to play and what Martin found it difficult to get across was the trauma his character was suffering. 'My own personality is quite the reverse,' he said. 'If I have a major problem on my mind I tend to bury it very deep and carry on without revealing my feelings. So my problem wasn't leaving the part behind at the end of the day but putting it on at the beginning. Though, obviously, you do go through that process of becoming the man you play and the role colours the way you feel. It's inevitable.'

Losing It certainly made Martin appreciate his own good

health and happiness. It made him more aware of his own testicles, too. And yes, he does check himself regularly, thanks.

The only aspect of the drama that didn't thrill him was seeing himself on screen. 'The older you get, the worse it gets,' he said. 'I get less and less confident about the way I look. I ran out of the room when I saw myself in *Losing It*. Mind you, being porky for the part was an acting choice,' he smiled. 'You know – even fat people get testicular cancer.'

CHAPTER 16

DOG MARTIN

'I am very happily and healthily obsessed with dogs.
I love meeting them and talking to them.
I swear I have dreams where I have a snout'
MARTIN ON MAN'S BEST FRIEND

When Martin left drama school in London, he could never have imagined that in pursuit of his art he would one day find himself sitting down at an upright piano to play *Chopsticks* in a roadhouse in the Australian outback to accompany an orphaned singing dingo called Dinky. Nor could he have envisaged himself willingly volunteering to be buried alive under three feet of freezing snow in the Rocky Mountains. Not to mention thrusting his nose into the mouth of a wolf in Devon.

'Never work with children or animals' is the advice frequently given in Martin's profession, but he couldn't resist the chance of fronting a two-part television documentary series called *A Man and His Dogs*. With it went the opportunity to travel in four different continents to meet, and literally rub noses with, various versions of man's best friend – including Dinky the singing dingo and Sula, a mountain rescue dog.

In fact, it was a project dear to Martin's heart. Such is his affection and enthusiasm for canines of all shapes, sizes and breeds, he regarded his participation in *A Man and His Dogs* as both a privilege and an enthralling adventure rather than a job of work. That much was evident to the millions of viewers who tuned in. 'I've been criticised throughout my life for thrusting my face into any dog's face,' Martin was able to say jovially, unashamedly and with a huge grin prior to the launch of the series.

Thanks largely to *A Man and His Dogs*, broadcast on ITV in 2008, Martin now enjoys a standing as a leading celebrity dog-lover. He would be the first to agree that his own three have contributed hugely to this reputation – especially his golden Cocker Spaniel, Mary, with whom he has appeared on TV many times, prompting such amusing admissions as 'She sleeps on my head.'

Endearingly, he refers to Mary Elizabeth, to give the animal her full name, as his 'first born', diplomatically pointing out that she arrived in the world a year before Philippa gave birth to their daughter Emily.

Also at home sharing Martin's love of dogs are Tina Audrey, another Cocker Spaniel, and Arthur Colin, a black Labrador frequently introduced to friends and strangers alike as 'the son I never had'. The assigning of two names to each dog is indicative of the high regard in which Martin holds them all. It elevates them from mere mutt status.

All three featured in *A Man and His Dogs*, notably Arthur Colin who endeared himself to viewers on his introduction to obedience class when he immediately rolled over and deferred to the collie next to him.

Given that he had the misfortune to be attacked when he was a boy of nine by two Weimaraners whose teeth drew blood, it's somewhat surprising how soppy Martin can be when it comes to dogs. 'I always worry that I'm a gushy bunny-hugger,' he fretted jovially while promoting *A Man and His Dogs*.

In fact, Martin partially blames himself for the unfortunate encounter with the Weimaraners, who lived opposite his family's home on Wimbledon Common. He approached them when his pockets happened to be stuffed full of biscuits, which prompted the dogs to lunge excitedly at his pockets and at his legs.

The experience did Martin no lasting harm either physically or mentally, and when his mother acquired a Jack Russell crossbreed called Jemima, Martin soon bonded with a dog for the first time. Jemima was acquired from an animal rescue centre principally as a pet for Martin's sister Amanda, but eventually Martin's affection held sway.

The first dog Martin acquired that he could genuinely call his own was a stray to which he gave a good home after friends had found it on Highbury Fields in north London, running aimlessly around and looking confused and lost. Coincidentally Martin was in the middle of filming *Gone to the Dogs* at the time, and he was living with his first wife Lucy in a garden flat in Tufnell Park, where Lucy's white West Highland terrier Charlie was also in residence.

'During the snows one February, friends of ours were out walking and this skinny dog with no name tag just attached itself to them,' Martin recalled. 'As they already had a big dog of their own they were unable to keep him. They were going to have to send him to Battersea Dogs Home but brought him round to me first.'

Martin was doing a spot of carpentry in the garden when his friends called round and introduced him to the stray. 'And when I saw this dog, our eyes met and that was that. I just said: "Let's keep him!"' he remembers. 'He was half hound and half Alsatian and we called him Angus.

'To begin with, he was terrible trouble, but he got better all the time. When we first took him in he had no idea of affection at all. He was a foxhound, which meant he wasn't the greatest of pets. If I was sad or miserable he would sit with me, but he wasn't one for being stroked. We used to stroke him and he'd look at us as if to say, "What are you doing that for?" There was a bit of jealousy at first because Charlie thought he was the boss, but as Angus could fit Charlie's entire head in his mouth, that kept him in check.'

Mary Elizabeth was the first dog Martin bought with Philippa. They acquired her as an eight-week-old puppy with some difficult health issues. 'Mary won us over immediately. She was gorgeous. She was the smallest, most demure puppy in the litter and she remains quite small and demure. Her history has a lot to do with that. When Mary was just four months old it was discovered that she had hip displacement and had to have three major operations to enable her to walk.

To complicate matters, Martin and Philippa were still living in their apartment in London, and house rules dictated there were to be no dogs resident in the block. At first Mary was small enough to be smuggled in and out unseen and taken up on to the roof of the building when nature called. Eventually her presence was detected by the doorman, but she was cute enough to melt his heart to allowed to stay. 'Fortunately Mary has always delivered with the "Aaahhh" factor,' says Martin. Now Mary enjoys the extensive acres of Martin's Dorset home with the family's other two dogs.

As followers of *Doc Martin* have come to know, Martin's character in the series has never been a dog lover – despite the appeal of Gremlin, the part bearded collie, part old English sheepdog who trotted around after the doctor whenever he got the chance. But once the cameras stopped rolling, Martin was the first to give Gremlin a hug and a few sweets.

Sadly Gremlin died in 2007, but *Doc Martin* viewers were soon introduced to Buddy, a Jack Russell whose real name was Dodger. He had come from the Dog's Trust charity after he had been found looking lost while walking the streets of Bradford. Dodger seamlessly arrived in a new series of the show as a little dog who was always trying to seek out Doc Martin and follow him home.

Dodger had no trouble gaining Martin's affection, and during breaks in filming in Port Isaac in Cornwall, Martin has been equally quick to befriend any dog that comes anywhere near him. And there is no shortage – Port Isaac's resident canine contingent is regularly swelled by the arrival of other pets brought along by their owners on holiday.

Naturally, filming draws an inquisitive crowd of onlookers and they rarely pass up an opportunity to introduce their dogs to Martin knowing full well he cannot resist stopping to give them a pat. 'People thought that, if they had a dog with them, there was a good chance I would talk to them. And they were right!

'One couple borrowed a dog from their friends because they knew I would speak to them. When I started asking questions about the dog, they confessed it wasn't actually theirs!

'With certain dogs I can get an endorphin-like rush when I see them. It is just their little faces, especially puppies, make me feel that I have to go up to them, which I don't think is uncommon. My wife thinks I was a dog in a previous life because I love them so much. I'm always greeting dogs and patting them in the street.'

Martin's enthusiastic greetings eventually inspired the idea for *A Man and His Dogs*. Rather than make a series about celebrities and their pets, the premise evolved into a worldwide adventure to delve into the history of dogs and to discover why the relationship between humans and dogs has lasted so long. 'When I look into the eyes of my own dogs,' Martin explained, 'I always find myself wondering the same thing: where did you come from?'

The project could have turned out to be little more than a self-indulgent travelogue with a canine connotation, but the two documentaries set out firmly to trace his pets' ancestry, with Martin displaying an endearing sense of wonder and curiosity.

The discovery that dogs are genetically still 99.8 per cent like wolves took Martin to America's Yellowstone Park to observe them in the wild feasting on an elk kill, and also to Devon, where he happily stuck his nose into the mouth of a wolf that had been reared in captivity.

Much of the appeal of the two programmes was the undisguised excitement Martin showed on his travels and his appetite for rubbing noses with a wide range of dogs. The sight of pure-bred wild dingoes frolicking in the dawn surf on Fraser Island in Australia took his breath away, and he crawled into a sub-zero snowhole high up in the Rockies as if he was a schoolboy gleefully discovering a secret den. Once inside, he lay giggling nervously, waiting to be dug out by Sula, the specially trained avalanche search-and-rescue dog.

Still in the Rockies, Martin was like a little boy granted a Christmas wish by Santa when he climbed on to a sled for a snowy joyride pulled by a team of huskies. And in the Malibu hills on the outskirts of Los Angeles he met Lassie, the greatest canine star of them all. Nine generations of the same collie family have played Lassie on screen and Martin was thrilled to be introduced to the latest in the line – real name Laddie – as he shot a commercial for charity.

In Boston, however, Martin was given a painful reminder that a dog's bite can be worse than its bark when a police dog nipped his ankle while he was taking photographs of her in training. 'I quite understood,' Martin said with instant forgiveness. 'I was taking pictures of her at the end of the training course and she was just excited and bit my leg.'

For Martin, a personal highlight of *A Man and His Dogs* was a return to the Mkomazi Game Sanctuary in Tanzania and a reunion with Tony Fitzjohn, 13 years after they had linked up for the release of Nina the elephant into the wild.

This time Martin was there to witness the release of seven African Painted Hunting Dogs, one of the most ancient of canines. Martin remembered seeing when he was a small boy a documentary about an African wild puppy called Solo. which had fired his imagination enough for him to read Hugo van Lawick's book *Solo: the Story of an African Wild Dog*. Ever since he had longed for a real life encounter and was rewarded when he'd met several on his first trip to Tanzania.

This particular group had been reared in captivity as part of a breeding initiative Tony Fitzjohn had set up some years before because of their dwindling numbers. There are now fewer than 3,000 in the world, whereas not so very long ago they numbered more than 200,000.

Martin was visibly moved when he slipped the catch on the pack's pen to allow them to race free into the bush. 'I opened the gates and let the dogs go into millions of miles of prime dog country. They never looked back. As soon as they went through the gate they completely changed their behaviour from when they were trotting around inside the enclosure they'd been born in. Tony had reared the pack from pups.

'What I learned from making the documentary is that I'm not alone in my love of dogs. With serious dog people I play down my unquestioning adoration of pretty much any dog. But seeing the Master of Hounds at Cattistock Hunt kiss one of the hounds, I realised whatever they say they are all as soppy as I am, however they couch it. Even hardened Tony, the wildlife expert setting big cats free all his life – he is really soppy!'

The return to the Mkomazi Game Sanctuary proved doubly poignant. While he was there, Martin was able to see the remains of Nina the elephant who had died some years earlier. 'That was very special to me,' he said. 'It was sad, but it was good I was able to say a final goodbye.'

CHAPTER 17

DOC MARTIN

*'There is a real liberation in playing a character who is
so rude that it goes against all the rules of society'*
MARTIN ON HIS ROLE AS GRUMPY DR MARTIN ELLINGHAM

Bad-tempered medic Doc Martin is now a popular
fixture on our television screens, with Martin Clunes
showing that he doesn't need to be playing Mr Nice Guy to
build up a big audience.

Doc Martin actually began his screen life as a much more
relaxed character in 2000's surprise hit film *Saving Grace*, a
comedy starring Brenda Blethyn and Craig Ferguson. Filmed in
the beautiful Cornish village of Port Isaac, this marvellous
movie had Blethyn as a woman left penniless when her cheating
husband leapt out of an aeroplane without a parachute. With a
huge house to keep up she joined forces with her crafty
caretaker, played by Ferguson, in a cunning plot to make money
to save her lovely home by growing cannabis.

Martin breezed into the film occasionally in a small
supporting role as the laid-back, dope-smoking GP Dr
Martin Bamford. The enchanting setting helped to make it a

successful film and Martin and his producer wife Philippa saw there was much more potential, both in his character and in the brilliant backdrop.

'I played the same character of the village doctor in *Saving Grace*,' said Martin, 'and in two films which were made afterwards for Sky. But we have changed him quite a lot for the TV series *Doc Martin* and we made the situation completely different. We have turned the usual rural doctor scenario on its head. Rather than have a doctor turn up among lots of strange village yokels and his discovery of them, which we felt had been done a lot before, we've got a completely horrible doctor with no bedside manner and he becomes the shared problem of the entire village.'

The name changed as well, as Dr Martin Bamford became Dr Martin Ellingham. The new name was an anagram of Minghella, the surname of the new writer Dominic (younger brother of the late writer-director Anthony, of *The English Patient* fame) who had been brought on board to help create a spectacularly grumpy new country medic. Some of Dominic's early work had been on the quirky BBC rural police series *Hamish Macbeth* and he was determined to give Doc Martin an unusual awkwardness that made him ignore many social niceties and frequently rub people up the wrong way.

Doc Martin was conceived and constructed as a star vehicle for Martin but when the writer softened some of the Doc's more abrasive edges to make him appear more lovable, Martin instantly objected. 'To his credit Martin said, "Didn't we say we would have a grump, taciturn doctor? This is not what you sold us," said Dominic. So everything went back closer to the original plan and Martin was happy.'

'There is a real liberation in playing a character who is so rude that it goes against all the rules of society,' Martin enthused.

Dominic said he was 'unbelievably excited' when he first saw some of his scripts on screen. 'I rang them up and said, "Let's book our tables at the award ceremonies now." It was already better than I had dared to dream. He inhabits the character. It is quite extraordinary.'

There were mixed feelings in the tiny village of Port Isaac when plans to make the ITV series were announced in the spring of 2004. Buffalo Pictures, the production company led by Martin and Philippa, knew that a good relationship with the locals was essential to a successful series.

Work on *Saving Grace*, and the two subsequent films by Sky, had tested the patience of villagers, who were not always delighted to see their lives disrupted by the paraphernalia of filming. So Buffalo held a public meeting in the village hall to give assurances that the intrusions would be kept to a minimum. The company agreed to avoid working at weekends and to try to cause as little trouble as possible.

From the start there was a very tight feeling between cast and crew. The star of the show tends to set the standards of behaviour on any production, and Martin's cheerful enthusiasm and hard-working attitude had a good effect on his workmates.

Martin believed that having everyone living and working together in that beautiful part of Cornwall had a hugely beneficial impact on the show. 'At the end of the day we would all go off and meet in the pub,' Martin explained. 'We even joined the pub quiz team on some nights. It was much better than working within the M25 where everyone just shoots off home at the end of the day.'

When the TV series began, we saw a very short-haired, smart-suited Martin playing the desperately uptight and unfriendly medic. He was an eminent and highly skilled surgeon who had been forced to give up his career in the operating theatres of London after developing an unfortunate but very powerful phobia of blood.

Forced to re-train as a GP, he had decided to settle in the sleepy Cornish village of Portwenn (as Port Isaac was called in the series). The story explained that he had spent many happy childhood holidays in the tiny fishing village and his Aunt Joan, played by Stephanie Cole, still lived there.

The new character was deliberately rude and unsympathetic. 'I can't wait. Bring it on!' enthused Martin during early preparations for the production. 'The Doc is horrible, with no bedside manner at all, but that makes him great fun to play.'

That startling lack of social awareness reveals itself very quickly on the flight to Cornwall for his interview for the post of Portwenn's GP. He stares so intensely at the attractive young woman sitting nearby that she moves away to another seat, snapping, 'You've got a problem' at the unsmiling medic.

With a certain dramatic inevitability the young woman (played by Caroline Catz) turns out to be a member of the interviewing panel. She is Louisa Glasson, a teacher and the lay member of the panel, and she is particularly tough with her questioning and dead set against his appointment. Outvoted, she challenges him angrily afterwards about his offensive staring, to which he retorts sharply that she needs to see an eye specialist as he suspects she has acute glaucoma.

Martin was in his element. 'It's so liberating to play someone who doesn't tend to like anyone or give a damn about what anyone thinks of him,' he said. 'I need approval all the time and usually play people who are desperate to be liked. 'I don't know where I got him,' he admitted. 'I don't even think he looks like me. But I do have a bit of a temper so I suppose some of that went in.'

In one early scene he had to shout at a woman to get out of the way. He yelled so angrily he made the poor woman jump and even the crew were surprised. 'Doc Martin goes out of his way to be offensive,' said Martin. 'And he looks a real fish out of water, too. He is always in a dark suit, even on a beach. I love him because he is so politically incorrect and says what he thinks.'

Interestingly, real doctors have advised the actor that Doc Martin is not being grumpy enough! 'Surgeons particularly have taken me to one side and said, "You're being far too nice for a surgeon."'

The first episode was a television master class in bad manners. Martin clashes with the removal men and refuses them a tip, then goes head to head with his brilliantly bolshie young receptionist. Roaring off in his Lexus, he comes across a couple of locals who decide that he is 'definitely Bodmin' and almost run him off the road. When he goes off to meet his Aunt Joan, colourfully played by Stephanie Cole, she can't believe he is now a fully qualified doctor and quickly reminds him that on his last visit when he was 11 he was a crybaby who wet the bed. She then strangles a chicken with her bare hands for their tea.

The bed-wetting line had echoes of Martin's own childhood and he was determined to include it as he felt it helped shape the personality of Doc Martin. 'I loved being loathsome,' smiled Martin. 'It gives you a great freedom. There was a scene in episode one where Celia Imrie says, "Oh, I keep forgetting things. It must be old age. Is there a cure?" And he just says, "No!" It's clear and it's truthful and it's quite refreshing to do that, but if you think he is nasty at the start, wait until you see how vile he becomes later on.'

The viewers loved it from the start. The first series drew over nine million viewers each week and was quickly voted Britain's best comedy drama. There was a real boldness about that opening episode, in which Celia Imrie plays an unfaithful wife whose liberal use of HRT cream has inspired breast development on the chests of both her husband and her lover. Doc Martin bluntly diagnoses the problem with maximum embarrassment for all concerned.

Doc Martin was definitely a show that dared to be different.

Martin said after the first series: 'It is a comedy drama but we don't think it's like the other ones.' With his wife Philippa as producer, Martin could exert considerable control and his sure feeling for comedy proved well worth listening to.

Martin had a very clear view of the level of rudeness he wanted. Many times he saw a draft and rejected it, saying, 'Oh no – take all the pleases and thank-yous out.' He was determined to be true to the original concept and produce this thoroughly crabby doctor. 'I always want people to like me,' Martin said, 'but Doc Martin is not like that. He has the surgeon's clarity of thought and doesn't waste time worrying about social niceties.'

The villagers are understandably shocked to have such a charmless GP and after they discover his phobia about blood they play a cruel joke. Plumber Bert Large, played by Ian McNeice, covers his arm in tomato sauce and the doctor is called to the pub so that everyone can see his reaction. When he erupts with anger the locals explode with laughter.

Doc Martin's volatile on-off relationship with shapely schoolteacher Louisa was central to the appeal of the show from the start. Martin laughed that some screen relationships invoke choirs of heavenly angels but there is a horribly raucous honk when the Doc and Louisa meet.

The couple are never quite on the same wavelength at the same time so the audience is forever kept guessing about the outcome. 'It's always awkward and tortured and we misunderstand each other at the drop of a hat,' said Martin. 'Well, I'm vile for a start, and she's lovely.'

Caroline Catz agreed there was a lack of communication: 'They always keep misunderstanding each other. She thinks she has got the upper hand, but actually I don't think she is as smart at handling the relationship as she thinks she is.'

At the end of the first series the couple share a kiss in the back of taxi after Louisa has witnessed Martin's medical brilliance as he saved a little boy's life. It is a rare moment of animal passion, but he blows any romance with his complete lack of social skills and his obsession for medical diagnosis at all times. After they break away Doc Martin can't stop himself asking: 'I assume you have a regular dental hygiene routine?' Very soon afterwards he is unceremoniously booted out of the cab by a furious Louisa, in a hilarious finale to a fabulous first series. 'His enquiry was quite well-meaning,' Martin smiled. 'Women are puzzling!'

In the second series Louisa has a fling with an architect who is a born again Christian, but they break up when he wants her to go to London. She gets drunk with Martin who tells her how beautiful she is before unromantically falling asleep. The producers knew that the will they, won't they factor to the relationship is what helps to keep the ratings so high.

From the start Martin gambled that even though the new doctor was deeply unpleasant to other people, and even to animals that got in his way, he could generate some sympathy for him. After all, the doctor had been a dedicated surgeon and he had lost the career he loved. 'There is a pathos about a man unable to do the one thing in the world he's brilliant at,' said Martin. And with no wife or lover in sight (at least initially), Martin made people feel for this uncomfortable loner.

Many of the production team were highly supportive and made the warmth of their feelings known in an illuminating 'behind the scenes' section on the official DVD release of *Doc Martin*, which has been a very popular seller.

Actor turned producer Mark Crowdy, the man who wrote the original *Saving Grace* story and some of the *Doc Martin* television series, had strong local connections. 'I'm really happy we've come back,' he said, 'because Port Isaac is its own character in this piece and it lends an enormous amount to it, as it did to *Saving Grace*. There was a lot of pressure to go somewhere closer to London, but we were determined to come back here.'

Director Ben Bolt said: 'Martin Clunes has a wonderfully eccentrically individual face. He is a very big man, which is quite funny on him for some reason. He is completely without vanity. A lot of actors will claim to be without vanity, but they are always keeping a weather eye out to make sure they are not looking too ridiculous. He doesn't care. He relies on you to shoot it any which way you want. He is wonderfully adaptable. He's got terrific stamina. He is hugely self-deprecating, but smart as a whip.'

Stephanie Cole (who plays Aunt Joan) says: 'He is a wonderful actor, Martin Clunes. He really is. He's not just a comedy actor. He is much more than that – he is one of our finest actually.'

Caroline Catz agrees: 'He is a brilliant actor and he

certainly makes everyone laugh a lot.' Ian McNeice summed his feelings up even more briefly: 'Mr Clunes steals it from everyone, being the supreme comedy artist he is.'

The good nature of the production certainly made an impact on its star. Martin particularly enjoyed the comedy side of Doc Martin. 'I don't like programmes where nothing funny ever happens, because I don't have a single day where nothing funny ever happens. I love to be with people who make me laugh as much as making them laugh myself.

'I also love the honesty of comedy. People go and see some awful turgid thing such as *The Duchess of Malfi* and fake their response. "Oh darling! It was marvellous!" But audiences won't fake laughter. If it's not funny they won't laugh, it's as simple as that.'

Martin loved working on *Doc Martin*, not least because it was not too far from his converted vicarage home near Bridport in west Dorset. He said he could drive home from the location in two hours and perhaps unwisely added that he had bought a device which told him where the speed cameras were situated. 'Unlike Doc Martin I am a real family man. I don't like being away from them for too long.'

Often Martin was accompanied on location by his wife Philippa and daughter Emily, and Cocker Spaniel Mary came along too. She even appeared on screen more than once. In the end they hired a cottage midway between Port Isaac and Tintagel to be together. 'Looking out as the sun set on the sea every night was fantastic,' said Martin. 'As a working experience it would be hard to rival.'

Mr and Mrs Clunes also visited chef Rick Stein's famous restaurant in nearby Padstow during the production. First he went so he could have a lesson in cutting up his own sushi, just the sort of thing Doc Martin would want to master. 'The school Rick has built there was fantastic and the head chef Paul taught me how to fillet and prepare sushi and mackerel and things like that,' said Martin. 'Then we were asked back to have supper with Rick and his wife and it's a fantastic restaurant. The food was really great.'

On a daily basis the cast and crew went to enormous lengths not to disrupt the normal life of Port Isaac any more than necessary. This was a consideration which was largely appreciated by the locals, many of whom benefited from the increase in business the TV series produced.

But there were critics who became irritated about roads being blocked during shooting and others who objected to Doc Martin being called 'a bit Bodmin' as a suggestion of mental illness. Some locals recognised the reference to Bodmin's history as home to St Lawrence's hospital and they were not happy about it.

Bodmin's mayor Harold Vanderwolfe, a former nurse at St Lawrence's, said: 'It's nasty. It's relating to the old asylum in the town and it's certainly not good for the town. Over the years a lot of work has been done to remove this stigma and this sort of thing doesn't help.'

Bodmin's rector, the Rev. Canon Graham Minors, agreed. 'No, that is not a nice thing to be said about Bodmin. Firstly, we live in an up and coming town – after a number of years of suffering from a lack of confidence. We don't need this sort of thing. And secondly, do we really want to be laughing at people with learning difficulties? They are harking back to years ago when it was acceptable and we don't live in that sort of society any more. I've worked with people with difficulties and I don't think they, or the parents of children with learning difficulties, would find it amusing.'

An ITV spokesperson, perhaps somewhat insensitively, replied: '*Doc Martin* is a light-hearted look at life in a fictitious Cornish village. We gathered that the phrase "going Bodmin" was common parlance in Cornwall and it was used to describe someone who stands out from local people. The phrase is directed at our leading character who really is a fish out of water in the village. We're sorry if people are offended by the content of our drama. It's a comedy and our intention was to make people laugh.'

While nationally the show was popular, the producers were disappointed that in Cornwall there was a degree of resentment among viewers. The *Cornish Guardian* complained that the series depicted the locals as 'half-witted morons'.

Martin wisely kept out of the arguments, but his success in *Doc Martin* added to his impressive standing as an actor and he remained in great demand. In fact, just after *Doc Martin* was launched, he was on television again starring in *Beauty*, Simon Nye's thoughtful re-working of *Beauty and the Beast*. 'It's one of three dramas on the theme of being trapped,' explained Martin. 'Tom Fitzhenry, the guy I play, is trapped because of his appearance. His face is severely disfigured through inbreeding. As a youngster he was teased mercilessly about his dodgy brow, manky teeth and red hair, so now he's stuck in a stately home in his own world. He falls in love with Cathy, a beautiful plumber played by Sienna Guillory.'

In the original story of *Beauty and the Beast*, the beast becomes handsome and wins the girl, but in this modern version Tom was left looking ugly (though Cathy falls for him anyway). Martin had to spend more than two hours in make-up to prepare for filming, but the idea of people ridiculing his appearance was one he could certainly identify with. 'People have always been very rude about the way I look,' Martin told the *Sun* newspaper. 'As a kid they used to call me names such as Dumbo because of my ears. So I can certainly empathise with the character.'

After an extended break that left *Doc Martin* fans feeling seriously deprived, the series returned to the screen in September 2009. After the wedding day disaster that climaxed the third series – both Doc Martin and Louisa get cold feet just as they are about to take their vows – there was enormous interest in the fourth series, which opened with a sensation that shocked the village.

Louisa returns six months pregnant to tell Doc Martin she is expecting his baby. The Doc is chatting with spiky old flame Dr Edith Montgomery – who had begun working at the local hospital – when his former lover arrives. It was a compelling start to the series and more than nine million viewers switched on.

'I imagine Doc Martin will cope appallingly with being a

father. And can you imagine the child, a little lad in a suit with fat ears, stamping round the Cornish coastline?' Martin said at the time. 'Will it soften him? He loves Louisa but he's just rubbish at love.'

Martin had deliberately chosen to take two years off from the series in order to spend more time with his family, to make the documentaries about dogs, and to film the revived *Reggie Perrin* comedy drama. But he always wanted to make another series, so he was particularly pleased to be back. 'I missed being in Cornwall for the summer,' he said. 'I do love filming in the village of Port Isaac because I know it looks gorgeous. As I drove back to the location, there was a sense of anticipation of being back there. We have been able to rent the same house just along the coast from Port Isaac where we have always stayed.'

However, he admitted that it took a while to get back into the character. 'Then suddenly you realise it is a sort of second skin and it is just lovely being back.'

The worldwide popularity of *Doc Martin* had brought tourists flocking to Port Isaac in the hope of catching a glimpse of filming. 'Every time you come back here there seems to be more and more people gathering to watch us filming,' Martin noted. 'People have come from as far away as Australia and New Zealand.'

But sadly one member of the cast was absent. Gremlin the dog, who stole the hearts of many viewers with his affection for the grumpy doctor, had died after the third series. The scruffy mongrel was replaced by a perky Jack Russell called

Dodger. 'He's a rescued dog from the Dogs' Trust charity and he is such a brilliant dog,' says Martin. 'He's called Buddy in the series and he goes to live with Auntie Joan, but he is always trying to seek the Doc out and follow him home.

'Dodger really is fantastic. He is good at his job and I like him. He will do anything. He will cock his leg up against you – without weeing, that is! And he will dig. We have had a lot of fun together. It is funny to me that Doc Martin doesn't like dogs because I think, "How ridiculous, not liking dogs!" I don't like people who don't like dogs.'

CHAPTER 18

NO MAN IS
AN ISLAND

'There is no way he is a nutter in my book.
It's brave and beautiful!'
MARTIN ON STUART HILL'S DECLARATION OF
INDEPENDENCE FOR THE ISLAND OF FORVIK

Martin approached his glossy three-part ITV documentary series *Islands of Britain* with great enthusiasm, but he never imagined it might plunge him into real danger.

The most frightening experience of his life came just off the Scottish island of Islay, which is surrounded by some of the most treacherous waters in the world. Some 270 vessels from ocean liners to submarines have come to grief here since records began, and it was while exploring this watery graveyard that Martin's enthusiasm for involving himself fully led him into trouble.

To illustrate the threat to shipping, Martin was keen to dive down to explore the wreck of a small steamboat called the *John Strachan,* which had sunk in 1917. The vessel – a Clyde puffer, a popular design at the time – was bringing vital cargo to islands in the Inner Hebrides when it hit a rock and went down to its final resting place. Mercifully all 80 members of the crew got off the ship and survived, but for a few scary moments Martin felt he was not going to be so fortunate.

Although his only diving experience had been in much more comfortable warm waters, he was keen to provide action shots for the camera crew. 'I'd never dived a wreck before,' he said, 'and the temperature of the water was freezing. I was worried about snagging my gear on something and getting trapped down there, but there are safety measures in place.'

But Martin had trouble with his mask. 'It quickly made me panic,' he said. 'I tried to stay calm and breathe properly but it got very scary down there.' He was swiftly brought safely to the surface by underwater minders in a dramatic sequence that instantly brought the cosy travelogue to life. 'It did look very ghostly down there. I tried not to panic, but they were the worst moments of my life. As I was coming up I knew I had to breathe sensibly when all I wanted to do was cry!'

In fact it was not Martin's first experience of the dangers of deep sea diving. He had first learned to dive while on holiday with his wife Philippa at Ambergris Caye, Belize's largest island. The couple had flown out for a romantic holiday early in their relationship and Martin could hardly have picked a better spot to learn to dive. Its crystal clear waters and the beauty of its 190-mile Barrier Reef, the second largest living coral reef in the world, have earned Belize a place among the top ten diving destinations in the world.

Since then the couple have been diving in the Maldives,

Maui in Hawaii, in Grenada and other areas of the Caribbean. But a dive in the waters off Bequia in St Vincent and the Grenadines turned out to be a scary affair when Philippa began to experience a tingling sensation in her hands and her elbows.

The local diving centre dismissed fears that there was anything wrong and pointed out that Philippa and Martin had nothing to worry about since they had not dived very deep. But when the tingling in Philippa's arms persisted, Martin decided they couldn't take the risk that she might be suffering from 'the bends' and hastily chartered a small plane to fly to Barbados. The plane had to fly at low altitude to avoid aggravating any problems Philippa might have and in Barbados she was put on a saline drip and given oxygen in hospital before being put into a decompression chamber for a few hours. It was a worrying time for them both but happily she emerged safely from the ordeal.

It was not nearly so scary for Martin with the camera crew around him in the cold Scottish waters, and the happy ending was one of many high points in a documentary series that was hugely enjoyable for both the presenter and his audience. It did involve a lot of travelling and staying away from home but family time is all important to Martin and he insisted on having at least a week at home after every week of island-hopping.

Martin's inquisitive good nature appeared well tuned to the difficult art of letting interesting individuals express themselves. In spite of his terrifying moment under the sea off Islay, making the series was a real labour of love for Martin. 'I've always been intrigued by islands,' he said, 'and how people have to constantly cope with the isolation of island life.'

The stylishly filmed series began at Great Britain's northernmost tip in the Shetland Islands, closer to the Artic Circle than London. There to reach the unmanned lighthouse on Muckle Flugga (which means 'large steep-sided island' in Old Norse), he sailed out in a tiny boat with local experts.

The lighthouse on the point where the Atlantic meets the North Sea was built by the father of Robert Louis Stevenson, writer of *Treasure Island*. But the 365 steep steps up to the remarkable building were anything but fictional. 'We had been told not to hang onto the hand rails,' Martin noted gravely. 'They are not safe because no one maintains them. I am scared of heights and I have this thing about vertigo, so it was quite an experience. It really did feel as if I was at the end of the Earth.'

Some production executives wanted to see the series full of exciting stunts that showed the actor's daring but Martin did not agree and said so. 'That wasn't my vision for the show at all,' he revealed later. 'I felt the people and the islands themselves were exciting enough not to involve manufactured jeopardy.'

Martin was as good as his word. He encountered many people who might have been considered eccentric, but he flatly refused to ridicule or patronise them. He seemed delighted to talk to Stuart Hill, a man from Bromley in Kent who has bought an island called Forvik – not much larger than a football pitch – which he has declared independent from Britain.

Mr Hill stamped the Clunes passport to mark his arrival and said that he was happy to recognise the Queen as his monarch. In fact he now styles Forvik a Crown dependency. But he flatly refuses to accept the authority of the British government as his research questions whether Forvik, or indeed the rest of the Shetlands, is really part of Great Britain at all. He has written to the Queen inviting her to make an official Royal visit but said sadly that he has yet to receive a reply.

Martin clearly warmed to Mr Hill. 'Some people will no doubt say, "There's this nutter on an island who has declared independence." But, to be honest, I think that he is doing an extraordinary thing and a courageous thing. There is no way he is a nutter in my book. It's brave and beautiful!'

Martin happily admits that he admires people who dare to be different, and he certainly met plenty of them. On remote Unst, which has strong Norwegian links, he was confronted by the island's newly elected leader, who was dressed like a Viking and appeared ready to do battle. But one smile from the cheerful presenter and the man admitted his name was Derek and showed that the natives were actually extremely friendly.

Martin was particularly taken by an unusual bus shelter

on Unst, where trusting locals had installed a comfortable armchair, fresh flowers, books and even a computer safe in the knowledge that no one will disturb them. 'It says something about island life that the bus shelter is not spoilt or vandalised as it would be if it were kitted out like this pretty well anywhere on the mainland,' said Martin.

Islands are different, he insists. They have a togetherness, a feeling of real community, that is very impressive. Martin particularly took to the Shetland ponies – 'We've got four of these little fellows at home. The foals are just adorable' – but what really impressed him about Unst was: 'the way the people of the island deal with their isolation through the sheer strength of their community spirit. It's uplifting.' And that is exactly how it came across to the viewers.

Martin revealed much about his own personality in his role as a celebrity presenter. On the relatively large joined islands of Harris and Lewis he was surprised to find religion still has a very strong hold, with church services attracting large congregations even though musical instruments are banned. In fact it was not so long ago that they padlocked the children's swings on Sunday. Martin admitted religion did not play a large part in his own life but was careful to respect the views of the islanders.

As a fervent animal lover, however, he was not so comfortable visiting a sporting estate where rich visitors pay to stalk and shoot deer. 'We have to keep low in case the stag shoots back at us,' he joked.

Martin had found a castle you could rent for £22,000 a

week, and even got himself done up in Harris Tweed with matching hat and trousers. 'It's important to look a tosser on these occasions,' he observed, with just a flash of the old Gary from *Men Behaving Badly* coming through. While accepting that the animals needed to be culled he still looked mightily relieved when the expedition out into the rocks and heather ended without a kill. 'As the son of a conscientious objector I am a bit of a novice with guns,' he said pointedly.

Martin met lots of fascinating Scots during the making of the programmes but the most famous one of all did not appear on screen. He bumped into Sean Connery when they changed planes at Edinburgh Airport. Martin told a reporter later: 'As we were getting our bags down from the overhead lockers at the end of the flight our eyes met across the aisle and I reminded him that I made a film with him. I was the funny-looking spy in *The Russia House*. He was so kind and pretended he remembered me.'

Life in the Scottish islands involves living with wild and windy weather. On starkly beautiful Eigg, Martin climbed the central volcanic peak with a cheery local guide nicknamed Scruff, who casually dropped into the conversation the fact that a powerful gust of wind had blown the roof of his house off a year earlier. Martin said later that he found the resilience of the islanders quite breathtaking. The people of Eigg had clubbed together to buy their island.

Perhaps Martin's favourite island is Barra. Golden beaches and blue seas combine to make a visitor think they are in the Caribbean, were it not for the fierce winds that whip across the landscape. 'Barra is officially the most beautiful place in Britain,' said Martin on television with some confidence. Though he did add that he was not at all sure how they measured beauty.

The residents seemed more concerned with the warmth of their community than the attractiveness of their surroundings. As one of them put it: 'Even when times are very hard and you think you want privacy, the whole island will come and wrap itself around you like a blanket and it is the most comforting thing ever.' Martin let the lady have the last word, not mentioning his own memories of his then-secret love affair with Philippa while they were working on the film *Staggered* 14 years before.

He moved easily on, dancing enthusiastically at the ceilidh, puffing bravely at bagpipes and working hard to create his own personal brand of whisky. It was only when he ventured further south to the tax haven that is the Isle of Man that the occasional critical note crept into the commentary.

Martin was happy enough to meet the genial shopkeeper who happened to be the prime minister. It was only when he shared time with a rich businessman who was a little too pleased with himself that a sharper note was allowed to intrude. 'I wonder if there's a Viking word for smug?' he mused.

Indeed Martin seemed most at home among the ordinary inhabitants of any island he visited. He positively revelled in his visit to the Channel Island of Sark with its lack of democracy and mediaeval form of rule, gleefully describing it as: 'the last feudal state in the Western world, where a man can beat his wife with a stick so long as it is no longer than his little finger.' He almost sounded as if he approved, so much was he enjoying his time on 'the island that time forgot'.

Martin loved the lack of cars and enjoyed learning to drive a horse and carriage, even though he bent the rules of his test quite shamelessly. The seigneur, as they call the unelected ruler of Sark, sadly explained that his right to sleep with any bride on her wedding day had been lost with the passage of time, like many of his other powers. Martin promised to return to the easy-going island, which is facing a political upheaval of its old ways.

By the time he concluded the series with a hair-raising helicopter trip to the top of Bishop Rock off Land's End, Martin seemed completely sold on the island lifestyle. Even having to use the tiny helipad on top of the 160ft-high Victorian lighthouse could not dampen his enthusiasm. 'I never used to suffer from vertigo,' he said. 'I spent my childhood up trees on Wimbledon Common, but since my daughter was born nine years ago I have started to worry about all sorts of things. I get this daft vertigo feeling. It doesn't completely freak me but it makes me feel very uncomfortable.'

Later he said reflectively that while he could never live permanently on an isolated island, he greatly admired the crime-free way of life of the smaller isles at least. 'There is a great spirit of independence among all the residents, particularly on the less well-off islands,' he noted approvingly. 'We all work hard for our families, but they also strive to keep their island alive as an entity, and I find that interesting.'

But he finished with a warning that while islands can create a real sense of community and strong feelings of identity, they can also be fragile and are often threatened by larger forces from beyond their shores. 'But whatever is thrown at them,' he concluded, 'Britain's islanders have an extraordinary capacity to adapt and survive.'

CHAPTER 19

REGINALD PERRIN

*'I think Martin Clunes is wonderful and he may save
the day, but I'm pessimistic'*
JOHN HOWARD DAVIES, PRODUCER OF THE
ORIGINAL THE FALL AND RISE OF REGINALD PERRIN

Abba were top of the charts with *Dancing Queen*, Jim
Callaghan had just become Prime Minister after Harold
Wilson's shock resignation, the Sex Pistols had caused a furore
by swearing on TV, Britain's James Hunt had just become
world motor racing champion, and there were just three
television channels in the UK when *The Fall and Rise of Reginald
Perrin* was launched on the BBC on 8 September 1976.

It was to become a comedy classic, one of the greatest and
best-loved sitcoms of all time. Given its reputation as a
masterpiece, there was therefore a sense of bewilderment
and shock in television circles when the BBC announced they
were to remake the series with Martin Clunes as the hapless
Reggie, a role which in the minds of millions Leonard
Rossiter had made his own.

Why tarnish the memory of an iconic comedy? Why
remake a series held so dear? These were just two of the

questions that immediately sprang to mind. There were many die-hard fans who thought it bordered on sacrilege for the BBC even to attempt it. And as for Martin, the general opinion was that he had either taken leave of his senses in believing he could step into the shoes of Leonard Rossiter or he was incredibly brave. There was no doubt he was taking a huge gamble.

With brilliant scripts by David Nobbs (based on his own novel), the original sitcom had provided television viewers with *the* rebel of the year: middle-aged, suburbanite office worker Reggie, ground down by the awfulness of life at Sunshine Desserts and trapped in a dull and impotent marriage to Elizabeth. Bored almost senseless by his daily grind, Reggie drifted off into a fantasy world which included envisaging his mother-in-law as a hippopotamus.

At work, Reggie was plagued by his ridiculously pompous, booming boss CJ (played by John Barron), a curmudgeon constantly declaring 'I didn't get where I am today by...' as his two sycophantic colleagues parroted 'Super!' and 'Great!' Reggie's daytime drudgery was enlivened only by his hopeless fantasies, mainly about secretary Joan, played by *Coronation Street*'s Sue Nicholls.

Dejected Reggie's ability to cope worsened every week and drove him inexorably to a midlife crisis, pushing him to the very edge until his only escape was to fake his own death, leaving his clothes on a beach.

By the second series anti-hero Reggie was a cult success as he went around under an alias, remarried his wife Elizabeth and founded Grot, a company selling rubbish at extortionate prices. Eventually CJ, the two yes-men and his son-in-law joined him in a commune dedicated to making the world a better place.

The series was such a hit with viewers that it even inspired its own entry in the dictionary: to 'do a Reggie Perrin' meant faking a suicide. By the time *The Fall and Rise of Reginald Perrin* finished in 1979 it had become one of the nation's best loved comedies. Critics and audiences alike loved it.

The incredulity that greeted the BBC's plan to resurrect the show after 30 years was therefore entirely understandable. John Howard Davies, the former BBC head of comedy who had produced the original series, went so far as to declare the new programme should be cancelled. He said: 'My initial reaction to this remake was the same as other people: why? I don't like remakes of programmes anyway. It's unimaginative. It's much better to start with a blank piece of paper.'

Davies, whose other successes include *Fawlty Towers*, *Steptoe and Son* and *The Good Life*, added: 'I think Martin Clunes is wonderful and he may save the day, but I'm pessimistic.'

However Perrin's creator, David Nobbs, believed that Reggie's dreams of escaping the rat race were as pertinent today as they were back in the mid-1970s. Commuting was just as difficult and frustrating, and in the credit crunch the lack of job satisfaction was as prevalent as ever, and the dream of escape was perpetuated by the proliferation of television programmes about buying a home abroad.

It was a feather in Martin's cap that he was the only actor approached about starring in the revival. He was told the BBC wanted to do for Reggie Perrin what they had done for *Doctor Who*. There were millions who had loved *Doctor Who* and they had greeted its return with unbridled enthusiasm. Martin, who was 14 and still at school when the original Reggie was on screen, hoped there was a similar appetite for his resurrection.

The key to Martin's acceptance of the role was the recruiting of Simon Nye to co-write the series with David Nobbs. Nye had written *Men Behaving Badly* and once he was on board Martin had no hesitation in signing up. Nobbs was perfectly happy to team up with Nye, saying: 'I couldn't do it on my own because I live in north Yorkshire down a track outside a small village, and I'm out of touch with office life and all the jargon.'

Rather than a remake of *The Fall and Rise of Reggie Perrin*, Nobbs and Nye wisely went for an update, a modern equivalent of the original. Instead of working for Sunshine Desserts producing exotic ices, Reggie now headed up the disposable razors section for Groomtech, a company making male grooming products – in an office just a few doors down from Sunshine Desserts.

Other changes included a younger, upstart boss called Chris Jackson (same initials), a new wife called Nicola – a harassed teacher (played by Fay Ripley) who has little time for Reggie because she has her own life to lead. While Reggie's mother-in-law was now missing, and therefore so was her image as a hippo, the new show saw the addition of Reggie's mother, played by Wendy Craig.

But there were a lot of similarities, especially in Reggie's marriage, which in 2009 had also lost its spark. The original Reggie had offered a series of inventive excuses for trains running late (and thus his own tardiness), ranging from an escaped puma at Chessington North to a badger eating a junction box at New Malden. The trains were still running late in the new series. The 1976 Reggie had also frequently complained that commuters in the packed carriages never talked to one another. They were still not talking in the update, but now they were transported in silence with earphones plugged in or working on their laptops.

The new series was recorded in front of a live audience and the laughter track not only gave it a whiff of nostalgia for viewers but reminded Martin of the heady days of filming *Men Behaving Badly*. Martin himself had laughed a lot when reading the scripts and found Reggie very likeable, kind and smart.

Crucially Reggie retained his vivid imagination. His romantic fantasies now focused on Jasmine (Lucy Liemann), the sexy new work colleague who is head of balms and lubricants. The first day Martin and Lucy worked together called for a very funny scene in which Reggie has a fantasy about playing naked table tennis with Jasmine. Martin admitted: 'It was one of those moments when you think, "This is a funny way to earn a living, isn't it?"'

Martin had decided he would not re-watch the original Leonard Rossiter episodes so that he could play the role in his own way. As writer David Nobbs watched the filming of the series and saw Martin growing confidently into the role, he was so impressed he was moved to say: 'My God, he's good!' He added: 'In my opinion the performances of Martin and Leonard Rossiter in the role are so good that it would be invidious of me to say one is better than the other.'

In the press build-up to the launch, Martin stressed he had been 'thrilled, flattered and honoured' to be asked to star in the show. He had been a fan of the original and he knew comparisons were inevitable as he stepped into Leonard Rossiter's shoes. 'They are really big shoes,' he said, 'and very daunting. But lucky me getting such a good job.' He exuded confidence in both himself and the project, saying: 'It's been one of my most enjoyable jobs for years.'

Predictably, the critics were divided when *Reggie Perrin* finally hit the screen. Sam Woolaston in the *Guardian* wrote: 'Anyone old enough to have known – and inevitably loved – *The Fall and Rise of Reginald Perrin* will throw up their hands and ask: why sully the memory of one of the greatest British comedies of all time? It was wonderful and unique in its time; a copy can only be disappointing.

'I feel sorry for Clunes: it's not that he's bad, it's just that he's not Leonard Rossiter. The show and he cannot be separated.'

Ian Hyland in the *News of the World* decided it wasn't funny: 'As a central character this Reggie is so unlikeable and unreachable you'd happily shove him in front of the next 8.16 to Waterloo.'

Andrew Billen in *The Times*, however, was full of praise for Martin and went so far as to say his portrayal was more amusing than Leonard Rossiter's. 'It is very funny,' he wrote, 'largely because of Martin Clunes as Perrin who lumbers through home, his daily commute and his office life like a giant suffering the early stages of pathological disinhibition.'

He concluded: 'Clunes must have been wary of stepping into Leonard Rossiter's shoes. He is funnier than Rossiter was in the part.' The TV audience seemed to agree. The series attracted around five million viewers and prompted the BBC to press ahead with plans for another.

John Cleese might be an entertainment icon, but when he spoke out disparagingly about the dire state of British television comedy programmes he inspired a sharp rejoinder from Martin. The *Fawlty Towers* star said that TV humour had been in the doldrums since the 1980s. Never afraid to speak his mind, Martin retorted that the same criticism could apply to Cleese himself.

'John Cleese certainly hasn't made any good comedy since the 1980s,' said Martin. 'Isn't it curious how successful people only think there's only success in their day? There's a lot of it about, unfortunately.'

Cleese had blamed the BBC, ITV and other TV companies for being too mean to pay the writers, and he said he did not believe the writers of today worked as hard or as well as they used to in the past.

Martin disagreed: 'There has been loads of good comedy. There's even loads at the moment. What about *Lead Balloon*, *Outnumbered*, *Pulling* and *Free Agents*? Sharon Horgan is a real talent and her fellow writer Chris Niel is amazing.'

CHAPTER 20

HOME ON
THE RANGE

*'The funny thing is, the happier I get at home,
the less I feel like dressing up for a living'*
MARTIN ON THE RURAL IDYLL OF HIS NEW LIFE IN DORSET

Martin first fell in love with Dorset when he attended a friend's wedding at Corfe Castle. With a thousand years of turbulent history behind it, the largely crumbled ruins of the castle, which was a royal fortress for 600 years, still manage to rise majestically above the Isle of Purbeck.

After the wedding, Martin and Philippa took some time to look around the area and were smitten by its varied coastline, its glorious scenery and its hamlets and villages tucked into rolling, unspoilt countryside. It prompted immediate thoughts about the possibility of buying a weekend retreat in the county.

It took two years of searching for the idea to come to fruition and when it did, the couple bought not some remote little cottage but a £750,000, six-bedroom, 18th-century former vicarage in the middle of a village called Powerstock. Among the former owners of the mansion was Field Marshal

Viscount Montgomery, the illustrious World War Two military commander.

The sleepy village, which has a river running through it, is situated in a steep valley on the edge of the Dorset Downs near Bridport. It consists of a few picturesque houses, a couple of inns, a church and a small primary school, and has a population of fewer than a hundred.

The new house was a first step in Martin and Philippa's plans to bring up little Emily in the countryside. Children tended to grow up so much faster in London, and Martin and Philippa felt the gentler environment of the country would offer Emily the chance to stay younger for longer. They were keen for their little girl to enjoy a full and proper childhood.

But the family were not destined to live in Powerstock for long. Inevitably word spread quickly of the television star's whereabouts and the family's home was easy to find for anyone who cared to try. In celebrity-obsessed Britain, there were just too many who wanted to do that. In the end Martin got fed up with people craning over the gate to snap pictures of a star's home. A loss of privacy was a price Martin had been paying since he rose to fame in *Men Behaving Badly*.

One day Philippa was out for a walk and came home full of excitement saying she had spotted the most wonderful farmhouse with outbuildings, landscaped gardens and fields. The house was set high up on a hillside near Beaminster, with a view to the sea 15 miles away. Philippa had fallen for it at first sight, as did Martin when she pressed her husband to take a look at it.

HOME ON THE RANGE

They decided they simply had to buy it, even though it would mean a huge upheaval and the selling of their house in Putney as well as their home in Powerstock. But they both felt it was worth it, and joy was unconfined when their purchase went through and they were able to move into their dream home in spring 2007.

They had not long settled in when Martin's mother died that September, with her son at her hospital bedside holding her hand. The pain, desolation and loss Martin felt in the immediate aftermath was partially eased by being able to contact straight away a funeral director he had worked with while playing an undertaker in *William and Mary*.

It was a comfort for Martin to be able to ask for the funeral director's help and advice, and he could also draw on the research he had done for his role in *William and Mary*. It stood him in good stead in his time of grief, and it meant that he at least had a grasp of a world about which most people know nothing and one they had to face when they were at their most vulnerable.

Daphne had been lovingly supportive of her son's career from the very start, something for which Martin will be eternally grateful. Her sometimes starstruck enthusiasm for every role Martin undertook had always spurred him on.

Martin owed her much, not least for sparking his love of dogs. In his book *A Dog's Life*, which he wrote to accompany the TV series on man's best friends, Martin's printed dedication was to his mother 'who didn't really care for dogs, but let us have one anyway.'

As with all actors, there is in Martin Clunes a need to be appreciated and loved. But unlike some, Martin is a man who never forgets those who have been good to him or shown him love and kindness. His reverence for Sean Connery is a prime example.

At the age of 19, Martin was a raw actor taking his first tentative steps into movies when he was given a small role as a spy in the 1990 film *The Russia House*. Connery was the star of the movie, and during the shoot the great man made a point of telling the youngster how good his performance looked in the rushes – the previous day's film footage.

This simple gesture of acknowledgement coming from a very big movie star made Martin's day. He knew Connery did not need to say what he did, and that what he said may not even have been true. But it was a kindly word of encouragement at a welcome time for Martin – and he's never forgotten it.

When Martin eventually formed his own Big Arts theatre company, he made a point of thanking Sean Connery in the programme notes for each of his productions. Apparently no one ever asked Martin why Connery warranted this very public display of gratitude, but Martin was pleased just to be able to record in print his thanks for a not-forgotten kind gesture.

Martin's need to be loved perhaps in some small way explains why he cherishes the unswerving, unconditional love of his dogs. They are without fail always pleased to see him. Whether he's just come home after a few weeks away filming or whether he's just come downstairs in the morning, the excited greeting he receives is much the same. Four-footed love and loyalty for their master is perhaps only to be expected, but Martin revels in it — and returns it in spades.

Given Martin's extraordinary popularity, some have wondered why Hollywood hasn't beckoned or courted him. But Martin's acting aspirations never amounted to a zealous thrust for fame. He has never been fiercely competitive — indeed he has never had much appreciation of football or other competitive sports. Similarly, he hasn't striven for the kind of star vehicle that many might have expected on the back of his undoubted ability and his proven bankability as an actor.

He admits he remains ambitious, but in recent interviews he has said that the more he enjoys his family life in Dorset, the less he feels inclined to work. Martin modestly prefers to point out that he has been lucky in the roles that have come his way. But at the same time, he does not covet, as he puts it, the kind of 'Tosser of the Yard' star roles where he plays the hero cop who solves the crime and comes out smelling of roses at the end. He has never been a man for violence on the screen and that view has hardened since he became a father.

Hollywood is likely to hold little allure now he is so happily settled in Dorset. His last foray was a limited role in *Shakespeare in Love*, which he enjoyed hugely. Never one to take himself too seriously, Martin was vastly amused that the costume department gave him a bigger codpiece to wear than the one assigned to Ben Affleck, something which he couldn't resist drawing to the American star's attention.

These days it would have to be a very special project to prise him away from his rural idyll. Any length of time away from his family and beloved pets would be painful now that he is such a contented homebody. Besides, he has less than happy memories of American involvement in one of his own film projects. He and Philippa had a stellar cast lined up for a movie, but to his dismay the project collapsed when the US backers pulled out.

While Hollywood may yet come calling for Martin as an actor, or possibly as a director, he continues to thrive and excel in television shows that mix comedy with drama. 'I never thought I'd work as much or the way I do,' he said recently. 'I'd have very happily settled for being a cheery character actor and, fortunately for me, I live in a country where we appreciate character.'

Given good scripts, Martin has proved time and again that, with the possible exception of David Jason, there is no British actor who treads more convincingly and expertly the fine line between drama and comedy.

The mini-series *Over Here* was, he believes, almost the perfect example of the ideal comedy drama script. Written by John Sullivan of *Only Fools and Horses* fame, *Over Here* explored the uneasy co-existence of British Spitfire pilots forced to share an airfield in 1941 with a group of green Americans, newly arrived with their B17 Flying Fortress heavy bombers.

HOME ON THE RANGE

Although the pilots are fighting on the same side, they clash constantly over girls and the idiosyncratic use of English by the Americans who, as the saying went at the time, were 'overpaid, oversexed and over here'.

Again showing the versatility for which he is noted, Martin played Group Captain Barker, in charge of the British squadron, and John Sullivan's script made for the smoothest of enjoyable acting jobs for Martin. 'Pretty much everything you do on television, you have to change the odd word or the odd sentence here and there to make it fit well,' said Martin. 'But I didn't have to with that. The key to everything was in every single word John Sullivan had written.'

For the role, Martin asked his mother for permission to borrow one of his dad's treasured pipes and he also grew a moustache to add to his distinguished look in RAF uniform. Perhaps with his father's anti-war views in mind, Martin was keen that along with the comedy, the television two-parter should show the horror of sending young men, at 18 little more than boys, up into the sky above Britain to engage in dogfights with the Luftwaffe.

'When we were filming, I sat in the cockpit of a Spitfire,' said Martin, 'and I found there are Volkswagens with thicker panels than those planes. They were so unprotected, and they aimed the guns by pointing the plane. Just incredible.'

Friends in Martin's profession are full of admiration for, and not a little envious of, the way he seems able to parcel up his time so successfully between work and family, as well as combining the two in carefully planned projects like *Doc Martin*. There Philippa is the producer, he is the star and they can film the series not too far from home and thus see their daughter regularly – and indeed take her with them on location along with the dogs.

'People say you shouldn't work with your partner, but I love it,' he says. 'I really respect Philippa's work.' The couple work together, says Martin, for the simple reason that they are at their happiest when they are together. 'When I met Philippa, I instantly recognised this as the relationship that was going to sustain me for the rest of my life.'

Over the past few years Martin, Philippa and Emily have scheduled their work so they have been able to return almost annually to Soneva Fushi in the Maldives for a family holiday. It is considered one of the most beautiful of the Maldivian resorts, and they have become such regular visitors to the island that they always stay in their same favoured room. Visitors to the Clunes' home have noted there is a picture of it pinned to their noticeboard, such are the cherished memories.

If this smacks of a creature of habit, Martin explains that holidays are so precious to him – as well as expensive – that he chooses to keep going back to somewhere he already knows, somewhere he's guaranteed a wonderful vacation for himself and his family, somewhere which provides the happiest of memories. Emily learned how to snorkel there, for instance, and how to ride a bicycle.

Martin and Philippa always plan something extra special

on their wedding anniversary. One year they stayed at the Villa San Michele, regarded as one of the most romantic places in the world. A former monastery nestling on a hilltop overlooking Florence, it is now a luxury hotel surrounded by trees and terraced gardens of lemon trees and roses. Another year they stayed at the Chateau du Domaine St Martin, a luxury hotel in Vence, high up in the hills behind Cannes and Nice on the French Riviera.

Anniversaries and birthdays are sacrosanct in the Clunes household. It is a measure of the importance Martin attaches to them that he reportedly turned down a role in the movie *Bridget Jones's Diary* because filming clashed with his wedding anniversary. He also turned down another role in *Lara Croft: Tomb Raider* because it clashed with his mother's birthday.

While he may now be a wealthy man, the old saying goes that charity begins at home, and it is certainly true for Martin Clunes. Every year he turns his homestead in Beaminster over to a fund-raising fair and according to the man himself, it has become 'one of the best and happiest days of the year'.

Buckham Fair at the Clunes' family home has become a highly successful country extravaganza after he and Philippa bought extra land next to their home. 'This is a way of saying a big yes to local charities,' says Martin. 'It started in a small way in 2008 when we dipped our toes with a horse show in aid of Riding for the Disabled. Even before we bought these fields, when we saw they were for sale I thought, "What a great place to have Buckham Fair." They are so beautiful and you can see across Beaminster and out to sea.'

Martin and Philippa chose Julia's House, a Dorset children's hospice, as the local charity to benefit from the 2009 event and sunny weather helped to ensure a bumper turnout. The Fair really came into its own with horse, pony and dog shows taking place alongside a funfair. There was also a busy beer tent, bucking bronco rides and all manner of stalls.

Afterwards Philippa told the local paper: 'It's been brilliant. Fantastic. It's exceeded our expectation. We've had loads of people here and we have raised loads of money for Julia's House. We have had lots of food and antique stalls and the dog grooming went very well, too. We've had face-painting and a stall with beer and champagne. We wanted to put on something for the children and they all seemed to have a really good time. The fun fair has been brilliant. We will definitely do it again next year.'

Martin wore a huge cowboy hat as he strode around overseeing the success of the show. 'I hope everyone has a great time and we raise lots of cash for a good cause,' he said. 'Hopefully the show will grow and grow each year. I get approached by an awful lot of local charities and I hate saying no to them. I genuinely hate it because there is no such thing as an undeserving or bad charity. So this seemed a really good way of raising a lot of money and having a lot of fun and easing my guilt.'

Martin explained that the fund-raiser was important to him because it combined his love of animals – particularly dogs and horses – with spending time with his family and helping people in need. Martin said he had all the passion of a 'born-again horse rider'. He first learned to ride as a child after being sent with his sister for lessons near Kingston-upon-Thames. But getting on a horse again was vital to him because his wife and nine-year-old Emily are now very keen riders. After building some stables he acquired his own horse, Chester, so he could ride with them.

At the show Martin said: 'I had to get a horse to join in some of the conversations being held in my house but I am very glad I did. I love it. Long after my lessons as a child I did some riding when I was working for Theatre Clwyd in North Wales. When you work in the theatre you have all day to yourself and because I was not at home one of the actresses was riding and it was so beautiful up there. I rode with what I now realise was complete abandon. I would go galloping along the Welsh mountains because you are invincible when you are 20, or you think you are!'

Martin's horses were among the attractions at the charity fund-raiser. He introduced visitors to Chester, the handsome old hunter he has learned to ride all over again. 'I have lessons whenever I can. Chester is the kindest "man" – he is absolutely perfect for me. He is 19 years old and he has got nothing to prove but he still has plenty of va-va-voom in him and he'll go. Emily has a gorgeous Palomino pony and my wife has a very pretty thoroughbred mare called Bee. Then we have four miniature Shetlands who are just stunning. They gave rides at the fair and they're all part of the family!'

The generosity of Martin and Philippa has impressed their neighbours and the couple are very popular in the area. Local businesses have rallied round with sponsorship and other help and the Clunes annual fund-raiser is now definitely on the calendar. But Martin still finds time to support a variety of other charities. Perhaps mindful of his father's death from cancer, one of the causes closest to his heart is the hospice movement. Martin made a moving video to help explain the movement in general and the work of Dorset's Weldmar Hospicecare Trust in particular.

'Hospice is a funny word, isn't it?' said Martin. 'It means something I am sure we all support. We might even think that we may need it one day. Unquestionably, it's a good thing. "That marvellous hospice care," we say, and how much we "admire everyone who takes part in it", and we mean it. But it's a sad word too, because however hard we try we can't help thinking that a hospice is the end of the line. But we really shouldn't because the important thing about hospice care is that it is not just about death. It's also about life: the quality of life and the enjoyment of life during what for many people can be a very long and rewarding time.'

Martin explained articulately how the hospice movement was about allowing people to take control of their own lives and making best use of whatever time they have left. 'Hospices are not just full of old people and cancer victims,' he said. 'There are people of every age undergoing treatment for a wide variety of conditions. So if you are one of those people who think that a hospice is the final curtain I am very happy to tell you that you are completely wrong.'

Martin was passionate about his message and determined to use all of his considerable communication skills to get it across. 'In Dorset hospice residential care is provided by the Joseph Weld Hospice where there are 18 in-patient beds. These are mainly occupied by people with motor-neurone disease or Parkinson's, multiple sclerosis or cancer or any of the other progressive conditions. But they are not death beds! Many of these patients only need a spell of nursing or extra treatment and once their symptoms are under control they can return home and pick up where they left off. Of course some people come back to die at the hospice, but only if that is what they and their families want.'

Martin was speaking in his role as a supporter of the Dorset Trust and he presented a warm and inspirational film that has helped enormously to bring in a considerable annual income, which the Trust needs to keep going.

Unlike many actors and celebrities, Martin does not hide away from his public. He is determined his fame will never isolate him from ordinary people and whenever possible he finds time to talk to fans. It was when he was talking to a couple watching shooting of the first series of *Doc Martin* that he became aware of the good work of HFT, a national charity which provides support for people with learning difficulties.

'I met this couple who were on holiday near Port Isaac,' recalled Martin. 'They told me that they were on their first holiday together in more than 30 years. They had been unable to get time away as a couple before then because their son had severe learning disabilities. They explained about the work of HFT and, as with so many of these things, I had not even considered that there was such a need, let alone a charity that could meet it. When I was asked to read at a fundraising carol concert at Truro Cathedral I was delighted to accept. HFT asked if I would consider becoming a patron and I was delighted to accept.'

Martin also energetically supports national charities like Macmillan Cancer Support and the Born Free Foundation, and happily confesses to bullying other people to help out as often as he can. 'It is great to be able to make a difference. I have been very lucky in many ways in my life and I know there are lots of people who have not been so fortunate. I'm more than happy to help out as often as I can.'

Close friends who have known Martin a long time are amazed at just how much he has changed over the years. They are pleased, and admiring too, at the transformation in the actor who was in real danger of going seriously off the rails when he was in his hard-partying twenties.

Much of the credit, as Martin happily allows, is due to Philippa. He met her when he was at a low ebb, battered and bruised from a broken marriage, and she has given him not only her love but a sense of direction and purpose in his career. She has also given him a daughter.

'You have never seen a more loving father,' reports a close

friend of the family. 'Martin absolutely adores her and it is wonderful to see them together. They'll go out riding together through the fields down to the sea and Emily will be chatting away with Martin listening attentively. He loves the fact that at this stage of her young life she has learned the names of different flowers, birds and trees and has a real feel for country life and nature, rather than how many Tube stops it takes to get from East Putney to Victoria.

'Philippa has become a keen vegetable grower amd Martin is thrilled that Emily can eat their own produce and see how it is grown, and can go for lovely walks in clean air. Martin is just crazy about Emily, and although he tries to be strict at times, everyone knows she can wind him around her little finger.'

Martin's devotion to Emily knows no bounds. There were times when she was small when Philippa had to go up to London on business and Martin was left alone with his little daughter. While his wife was away, Emily took to sleeping in Martin's bed and he developed an irrational fear that he would die in his sleep.

While tossing and turning in bed, he listened to his pulse beating through the pillow and became so convinced it was an irregular beat that he took himself off to the doctor – who told him he was worrying over nothing. 'But for a time,' he said, 'I was terrified I was going to die and leave my wife without a husband and Emily fatherless. I had this great fear of Emily waking up in the morning and finding her dad lying dead beside her.'

Martin likes to describe his family as 'the perfect gang of three'. It's interesting to note that for much of his childhood he was also a gang of three with his sister Amanda and his mother Daphne after his father died. As then, he is now the only male of the three – apart from Arthur Colin, the black Labrador. It is no coincidence that Martin provided the voice of Merlin, a lovable black Labrador with a magic collar in the animated series *Merlin the Magical Puppy*. His was also the voice of Kipper, a cartoon dog based on the children's books by Mick Inkpen.

Today Martin's life could not be more different from the hard-partying young actor of 20 years ago who would regularly wake up with a hangover. 'I'd wake up and if I didn't have a cigarette I'd get this feeling that there were two thumbs behind my eyeballs trying to push them out, and I'd get blurry and feel so ill. The first cigarette made me feel iller still before I'd be up and running.'

Today Martin is a reformed smoker, determined to be a father to Emily for longer than his own dad was able to be a father to him. 'When Emily has children one day, I want to know them,' he says poignantly. In Dorset, his day now starts with a bracing intake of fresh country air rather than cigarette smoke.

He's usually up at 6.30 ready to feed his chickens, all of whom have very grown-up names, Maisie the cat and the dogs, not forgetting to fill up the haynets of his horses and check on the 16 fish that have joined his menagerie. These days Martin wouldn't have it any other way. 'The funny thing is, the happier I get at home the less I feel like dressing up for a living,' he said recently. But, with a mortgage to pay he knows he will keep at it.

In recent years it has crossed Martin's mind that his face has become so familiar on the nation's television screens that the public might get fed up with him. He is aware, too, that if he appears on screen too often as himself it might be harder for him to convince the public he is someone else when it comes to dramatic roles.

As yet there appears no danger of that. The audience ratings for *Doc Martin* remain consistently high and his documentary series about dogs was so popular that a similar series about horses is in the pipeline. He has skilfully juggled both his acting work and his documentaries to make sure there are enough months in the year when television is a Clunes-free zone.

In 2007, Martin officially became Doc Martin when Bournemouth University awarded him the honorary degree of Doctor of Arts for his work in acting, thus making him a real-life Doctor. Dressed in a blue cap and gown and grinning widely, Martin received loud and warm applause from graduates when he was handed his scroll. He made a short speech saying how flattered he was before adding: 'I can't help feeling I've nicked something. It only occurred to me a while after I found about this that I would in fact be Doc Martin.'

Charles Elder, spokesman for Bournemouth University, said they were honoured the actor had accepted the degree.

He said: 'Martin has achieved such a lot what with his successful career and his own production company. He has also adopted Dorset as his own county and devotes a lot of time to charity here.'

These days Martin is in the enviable position of being able to pick and choose his roles and work when he wants to. And he has a clear vision of what he does for a living. 'I know what I want from this acting game,' he has said. 'I want it to be enjoyable. I also know what I don't like about it. I don't like the kind of actor who reckons he is an oracle who must be listened to. I dislike people who are trying to be self important.' Without belittling the art of acting, he says that by and large what he does is quite intangible. 'You turn up, dress up, ponce about a bit, it gets squirted through the airways and you're done.'

Growing up as an actor, Martin never dreamed he would one day have the life he has now. He's surprised to be a man of property, happily married with a beautiful daughter living a Thelwellian life in the Dorset countryside in a magnificent farmhouse set amid glorious surroundings. 'I have been very lucky,' he says. 'When I look back at everything, I never saw any of this coming and I am incredibly grateful.'

The family's 135 acres of garden, fields and woods are a far cry from the flat Martin shared with Philippa in London and provide the privacy that was lacking at their previous Dorset home. Any spare time he gets Martin likes nothing better than to go into his workshop to plane a block of wood and use his carpentry skills to make a door for a new fruit cage, a wooden box, or a piece of furniture. He says his most treasured possession is a piece of furniture – a grandfather clock that belonged to his grandfather, made in Suffolk in the 19th century.

Martin finds carpentry immensely satisfying, though he did once cut the top of a finger right to the bone in his woodwork studio. He rushed to the freezer to get some ice while shouting for help to Philippa, who drove him to hospital.

Martin also likes to spend time in the studio he has had built in the cottage where he can record voiceovers, lay down guitar tracks if the mood takes him and experiment with his vast, constantly updated collection of different sounds. Amassed over the years, his audio library includes everything from barking dogs to birdsong to eerily creaking gates.

Martin also likes to tinker with an old camper van he has been restoring for many years. As a millionaire, he could quite comfortably afford to buy the latest Ferrari or Bentley if the mood so took him – perhaps a stylish new Aston Martin would be even more appropriate. But the easy-going actor is unlikely to be seen at the wheel of anything so brash or flamboyant – his choice is of one of his lovingly restored, functional VW camper vans. There's no power steering so every drive is a long haul and they are so slow that they accelerate from 0 to 60 in a weekend.

A motor fan, Martin has owned several VW campers over the past few years but when waxing lyrical about them in 2004 he had two garaged safely on his country estate.

'There's something so self-contained about a VW camper,' he told the *Sunday Times*. 'They are not as annoying to be stuck behind as a caravan because they are shorter and easier to overtake. And it changes your personality: it's like a land barge, especially round the lanes. You can even see over the hedges. They always start first time and because it won't go fast you go slowly and enjoy the view.'

Martin bought a prized black 1968 model at an auction at Beaulieu and has used his carpentry skills to restore it to its former glory. The auctioneers said they had more interest in the camper than in all the stylish vintage sports cars lined up alongside it. Martin was determined to win the day even after the bidding went past the £5,000 guide price and was victorious in the end. 'It was one of the most exciting days of my life,' he said afterwards.

Martin is very conscious of the friendly image of the VW camper and enjoys the smiles of other road users who beam at such an ageing gentleman of the road. Martin also has a much higher performing people-carrier in the shape of a gleaming Toyota Land Cruiser. 'Driving that is how to be really loathed,' says Martin. 'People hate them and hate meeting you on the roads. But they love the camper; it cheers people up – you see them smiling at you.'

Being self-employed, Martin has always been cautious about spending too much money on cars. But the level of his success allowed him to relax a little and he bought a very large and very fast BMW, a 645Ci coupe. 'I've always loved coupes,' he said, 'and I've decided that BMW stands for Big

Menopausal Wanker. What makes me use the word menopausal is that I usually loathe sports cars because of being 6ft 3in, but what is a coupe if not a kind of fat boy's sports car?'

Horribly teased as a small boy for his large ears and lips, Martin is having the last laugh on the bullies. Along the way he has had to endure unflattering comments from critics about his looks, and he has largely silenced them too with his success. He thanks his lucky stars that he never took up Jeremy Brett's offer to pay for an operation to have his ears pinned back. 'I considered it for a while, but in the end I thought that was the shape I was born, and that was the shape I would stay.

'Boy, was that the right decision! Imagine taking away the very things that have become my greatest asset.'

Asked if there was anything about his career which he regretted, Martin shot back: 'No. I've been incredibly lucky, much luckier than I ever dreamed possible.'

CAREER HISTORY

MAJOR TV APPEARANCES

DOCTOR WHO (BBC)
First broadcast: 1983
Martin had a small role as the villain Lon in a four-part story called *Snakedance*, which starred Peter Davison as the time traveller.

NO PLACE LIKE HOME (BBC)
First broadcast: 1983
Sitcom starring William Gaunt and Patricia Garwood as a couple looking forward to some peace and quiet after their children have left home – until they find all the kids back living with them. Martin played their teenage son Nigel who had a different girlfriend every week.

GONE TO THE DOGS (ITV)

First broadcast: 1991

Comedy drama series centred around dog racing, with Jim Broadbent as an ex-con whose get-rich-quick schemes always fail and Warren Clarke as a successful video shop entrepreneur, both trying to end up with lovely Lauren (Alison Steadman). Martin appeared in six episodes as the accountant Pilbeam.

MEN BEHAVING BADLY (ITV and BBC)

First broadcast by ITV: 1992

First broadcast by BBC: 1994

Defining sit-com of the 1990s following the lives of Gary and Tony, two loveable but uncouth, lager-swilling flatmates, played by Martin and Neil Morrissey. Caroline Quentin and Leslie Ash co-starred as their long-suffering girlfriends Dorothy and Deborah. First screened on ITV with Harry Enfield as Martin's flatmate, *Men Behaving Badly* became a massive hit after Morrissey replaced Enfield and the show was switched to the BBC after being cancelled by ITV. A total of six series were made, as well as a Christmas special and three feature-length final episodes.

AN EVENING WITH GARY LINEKER (BBC)

First broadcast: 1994

Comedy television movie based on the play about British tourists in Majorca watching the 1990 World Cup. Clive Owen starred as Bill, desperate to watch England play

Germany on TV, with Caroline Quentin as his bored wife Monica. Joining them to watch the game are Bill's annoying friend Ian (Paul Merton) and Dan (Martin Clunes) whom Monica has secretly been seeing.

OVER HERE (BBC)
First broadcast: 1996
The title for this two-part mini-series was taken from the derisive description of the American military and airmen based in England during World War Two: 'overpaid, oversexed and over here!' Martin starred as British liaison officer Captain Baker, who presides over the friendly rivalry when Brits and Yanks are forced to live in the same barracks. Samuel West co-starred.

TOUCH AND GO (BBC)
First broadcast: 1998
Martin and Zara Turner played a married couple whose sex life has gone stale and decide to visit a wife-swapping club in a bid to reinvigorate their marriage. But after initial positive effects, the very basis of their marriage is placed under threat.

NEVILLE'S ISLAND (ITV)
First broadcast: 1998
Martin played Roy, one of four white-collar businessmen who undertake a team-building exercise but disaster capsizes their boat and delivers them to an uninhabited island in the Lake District. Stripped of the creature comforts they are all

accustomed to, they must learn to fend for themselves and face up to the realities of the natural world. With Timothy Spall, Jeff Rawle and Sylvia Sims.

SEX 'N' DEATH (BBC)
First broadcast: 1999

Martin took on the role of Ben Black, host of a popular television programme for whom nothing is too vulgar, distasteful or shocking – for his guests or his audiences – provided it improves his ratings. In his pursuit of viewers he offers £5,000 to the first member of his audience to strip naked, invites the world's major religions to settle their differences in a mud-wrestling match, and places live crabs down contestants' underpants. Martin Jarvis co-starred as his TV rival.

HUNTING VENUS (ITV)
First broadcast: 1999

Director: Martin Clunes

Feature-length comedy movie which has become a cult favourite. Former New Romantics pop star Simon Delancey (Martin Clunes) is kidnapped by two fans of his 1980s band the Venus Hunters and blackmailed into re-forming the band for one final gig. Neil Morrissey co-starred as a band member who has become a transsexual called Charlotte, with Jane Horrocks as a besotted fan.

CAREER HISTORY

LORNA DOONE (BBC)

First broadcast: 2000

Two-part adaptation of RD Blackmore's classic novel about feuds, revenge and star-crossed love in 16th-century England. Amelia Warner starred as Lorna, whose romance with young John Ridd (Richard Coyle) is imperilled by the long-standing feud between their families. Standing strong among the pillaging and terrorising in the Exmoor countryside is the redoubtable Jeremy Stickles (Martin Clunes).

DIRTY TRICKS (ITV)

First broadcast: 2000

Salacious comedy drama starring Martin as Edward, an unscrupulous English tutor at a seedy language school in Oxford. On the surface Edward is charming, witty and accomplished, but underneath this veneer is a calculating liar and manipulator. A dinner invitation leads him to some serious money and down a precarious path.

GORMENGHAST (BBC)

First broadcast: 2000

Ambitious £10million version of Mervyn Peake's Gothic fantasy trilogy, which focuses on life in the eponymous castle, ruled by the Groan family for more than 70 generations. Martin played Professor Flower.

A IS FOR ACID (ITV)

First broadcast: 2002

Fact-based drama with Martin playing the notorious real-life 1940s serial killer John Haigh, who earned himself a place in crime history as the Acid Bath Murderer. Haigh was a successful engineer and socialite, but his veneer of respectability hid murderous tendencies and he embarked on a cold-blooded killing spree, believing no trace of his victims would remain if he disposed of their bodies in vats of acid. He was caught only when the gallstones of one of his victims failed to dissolve. Keeley Hawes and Celia Imrie also starred.

GOODBYE MR CHIPS (ITV)

First broadcast: 2002

Television adaptation of James Hilton's novel about a schoolmaster who devotes his life to generations of schoolboys. Martin starred as the much loved Mr Chipping in a story spanning the 50 years from his arrival at Brookfield School in 1880 as an earnest young Latin master, through the turmoil of World War One to his last days in the 1930s. By this time he has become a legend, having earned the respect and love of the boys in his charge.

WILLIAM AND MARY (ITV)

First broadcast: 2003

Romantic comedy drama following, over three series, the search for love and the perfect partner by William Shawcross (Martin Clunes), a widowed undertaker, and midwife Mary

Gilcrest (Julie Graham) after they meet via a dating agency. As they fall in love, they face various challenges which test their devotion to each other, not least from their respective jobs dealing with life and death.

DOC MARTIN (ITV)
First broadcast: 2004
Comedy drama starring Martin as a grumpy GP with no semblance of bedside manner. Doctor Martin Ellingham takes a post in a sleepy Cornish hamlet after moving from London where he was a brilliant surgeon until he developed a phobia of blood. His prickly manner, his dislike of dogs and his habitual failure to understand other people make for a prickly relationship with the community.

LOSING IT (ITV)
First broadcast: 2006
Comedy drama about the impact on family and work life of fortysomething advertising executive Phil McNaughton when he is diagnosed with testicular cancer. Phil and his wife Nancy (Holly Aird) have to put on a brave face for the sake of their two children.

THE MAN WHO LOST HIS HEAD (ITV)
First broadcast: 2007
Two-hour drama shot in New Zealand with Martin playing highly serious museum curator Ian Bennet. About to marry his boss's daughter, he finds his life turned upside down

when he is sent across the world to return an ancient Maori carving to a small New Zealand town on the coast of North Island. Also starred Caroline Harker.

REGGIE PERRIN (BBC)
First broadcast: 2009
Modern update of the classic 1970s sit-com. Martin re-created the role made famous by Leonard Rossiter of a middle-aged executive fed up with the daily grind of commuting on overcrowded trains to an office where he has to contend with two fawning junior executives and an overbearing boss. Lacking attention from his wife, Reggie finds a fantasy distraction in a comely colleague called Jasmine.

MOVIES

THE RUSSIA HOUSE (1990)
Thriller based on John Le Carre's espionage novel, with Sean Connery as Barley Blair, a hard-drinking London publisher who receives a highly sensitive manuscript via Moscow editor Katya (Michelle Pfeiffer). Intercepted by the British authorities, the text purports to lay out Soviet nuclear capabilities in devastating detail. Blair is sent to Moscow to determine the text's reliability. Martin had a small role as a spy called Brock.

THE BALLAD OF KID DIVINE (1992)

Spaghetti western spoof featuring Neil Morrissey and Martin as two bounty hunters out to track down a wanted killer with a baby face and a $25,000 price on his head. Jesse Birdsall played Kid Divine.

STAGGERED (1994)

Director: Martin Clunes

Comedy starring Martin as husband-to-be Neil Price, whose stag night is sabotaged by his scheming best friend Gary (Michael Praed). After Gary spikes Neil's drink and dumps him unconscious and naked on a remote Scottish island, Neil has to embark on a road trip to get back to his fiancée before Gary gets a hold on her heart and her chequebook.

SHAKESPEARE IN LOVE (1998)

Romantic comedy centred on a young William Shakespeare, out of money and bereft of ideas, who is inspired to write by his forbidden love for Viola de Lesseps, a noble woman played by Gwyneth Paltrow. Martin had a small role as actor and theatre owner Richard Burbage. The film won seven Oscars.

MAJOR DOCUMENTARIES

AN ELEPHANT CALLED NINA (BBC)

First broadcast: 1997

Martin travelled to Tanzania to help with the release back into the wild of an elephant that had been kept in a zoo for 27 years.

MEN DOWN UNDER (BBC)

First broadcast: 2000

Three-part documentary in which Martin and his *Men Behaving Badly* co-star Neil Morrissey embarked on a tour of Australia in search of the essence of the Aussie male. Together they followed the route of the Olympic torch and finished their tour by visiting Surfer's Paradise on the Gold Coast, watching an Aussie Rules game in Melbourne and taking in Sydney's gay and lesbian Mardi Gras.

BEARS BEHIND BARS (Animal Planet)

First broadcast: 2001

Martin followed the efforts of crusader Victor Watkins to combat the barbaric treatment of bears forced to live in squalid confinement in Japanese bear parks, in conditions so bad they cannot even stand up.

CAREER HISTORY

MARTIN CLUNES: A MAN AND HIS DOGS (ITV)
First broadcast: 2008

Two-part documentary in which Martin set off on a worldwide adventure to discover why the relationship between humans and dogs has lasted so long. On his travels Martin met dingos in Australia, African wild dogs in Tanzania, rat-catching Jack Russells in Kent and a snow rescue dog in the Rockies, as well as observing wolves in the wild in Yellowstone Park.

ISLANDS OF BRITAIN (ITV)
First broadcast: 2009

Three-part documentary series in which Martin explored some of the thousand islands off Britain's coast. His travels took him from the most northern tip of the country to its southerly seas to find out what life is like for people who choose to live and work away from the mainland.